THE *Total* MONEY MAKEOVER

Transform!

Romans 12:2

Other Books from Dave Ramsey

The Total Money Makeover Workbook

The Total Money Makeover Journal

The Total Money Makeover Spanish Edition
(La Transformación Total de su Dinero)

EntreLeadership

Dave Ramsey's Complete Guide to Money

Smart Money Smart Kids
(with Rachel Cruze)

Foundations in Personal Finance
(K-12, College, and Homeschool)

Tranquilidad Financiera
(Spanish Edition of *Financial Peace*)

More Than Enough

The Legacy Journey

Junior's Adventures
(Children's Series)

Baby Steps Millionaires

THE *Total* MONEY MAKEOVER

A PROVEN PLAN *for* FINANCIAL PEACE

EXPANDED AND UPDATED EDITION

DAVE RAMSEY

NELSON
BOOKS

An Imprint of Thomas Nelson

The Total Money Makeover: A Proven Plan for Financial Peace, Expanded and Updated Edition

© 2003, 2007, 2009, 2013, 2024 by David L. Ramsey III

Published in Nashville, Tennessee, by Nelson Books, an imprint of Thomas Nelson. Nelson Books and Thomas Nelson are registered trademarks of HarperCollins Christian Publishing, Inc.

Thomas Nelson titles may be purchased in bulk for educational, business, fund-raising, or sales promotional use. For information, please email SpecialMarkets@ThomasNelson.com.

Scripture quotations marked NKJV are taken from the New King James Version®. Copyright © 1982 by Thomas Nelson. Used by permission. All rights reserved.

Scripture quotations marked CEV are taken from the Contemporary English Version. Copyright © 1991, 1992, 1995 by American Bible Society. Used by permission.

Scripture quotations marked NIV are taken from the Holy Bible, New International Version®, NIV®. Copyright © 1973, 1978, 1984, 2011 by Biblica, Inc.™ Used by permission of Zondervan. All rights reserved worldwide. www.Zondervan.com. The "NIV" and "New International Version" are trademarks registered in the United States Patent and Trademark Office by Biblica, Inc.®

ISBN 978-1-4003-4252-5 (hardcover)
ISBN 978-1-4003-4255-6 (eBook)
ISBN 978-1-4003-4254-9 (audio)

The Library of Congress has cataloged the earlier edition as follows:

Ramsey, Dave.
   The total money makeover : a proven plan for financial fitness / Dave Ramsey.
     p. cm.
   ISBN 978-0-7852-8908-1 (2007 edition)
   1. Finance, Personal. 2. Debt. I. Title.
   HG179.R31563 2003
   332.024'02—dc21   2003014115

Printed in the United States of America

24 25 26 27 28 LBC 5 4 3 2 1

To my beautiful wife, Sharon, who walked arm in arm with me through a Total Money Makeover—I love you, honey.

To the superstars all across America who have had the courage to face the person in the mirror, the culture, their family, and even their coworkers as they "lived like no one else so later they could live like no one else." You who have courageously had a Total Money Makeover of the heart and wallet are the real superstars.

To the Ramsey Solutions team and the Thomas Nelson team for tireless hours on this project to make this material available to everyone across this great land.

Contents

Introduction

Read the stories of the lives changed by this book! As a matter of fact, I recommend you skip through the book, reading all the stories first. They will inspire you to read all the way through and actually do the Proven Plan to Financial Fitness.

Many years ago I was given a calling: to show people the truth about debt and money and to give them the hope and tools necessary to set themselves free financially. First, I did that with a few speaking engagements and a small self-published book titled *Financial Peace*. Later *Financial Peace* was published by a New York publisher and became our first *New York Times* bestseller. I began doing a small local radio show that's now carried by hundreds of stations across the nation, as well as on podcast platforms like YouTube and Spotify. All that adds up to millions of listeners and viewers who tune in weekly. Thirty years ago, we started teaching a class called *Financial Peace University*, which millions of families have now attended. Then came *The Total Money Makeover*.

I am positive that personal finance is 80 percent behavior and only 20 percent head knowledge. Our concentration on behavior—realizing that most folks have a good idea of *what* to do with money but not *how* to do it—has led us to a different view of personal finance. Most financial people make the mistake of trying to show you the numbers, thinking that you just don't get the math. I am sure that the problem with my money is the guy in my mirror. If he will behave, he can make the money thing work. The math of wealth building is not rocket science; it is simple—but you have to DO IT!

So the proven Total Money Makeover plan I teach has become very successful not because I have found the secrets of the rich. Not because I had some revelation that no one else has ever had about credit cards. Not because I am the only one with a debt snowball plan. Instead, this proven plan is having a national impact because I have realized that to change your money thing, *you* have to change. You have to change your life. When you change your life, you will get out of debt, give, and invest at an unbelievable rate. When you read the stories in this book, you will read not about mathematics or magic systems, but about changed lives. You will read about transformed marriages and relationships. Because when you change your life, you really change your life.

So when Mike Hyatt, then the president and CEO of Thomas Nelson Publishers, brought me the concept for a *Total Money Makeover* book, I became very excited. I became excited because I knew this book would inspire readers to take immediate action through a simple, step-by-step process that could only lead to life-changing results. Hope—the light at the end of the tunnel that is not an oncoming train—is a very powerful force.

As excited as I was, though, I had no idea at the time what we were starting. I thought this stuff was common sense, but it turns out common sense isn't that common anymore. This book hit the market like a light-ning bolt—it just blew up! And it wasn't because I was some genius; it was because the country was ready for a financial wake-up call. It was because American families—hard-working men and women who were sick and tired of being sick and tired financially—were ready to change their lives. Looking back now, over a decade later, I'm blown away at what these people have accomplished, and I'm humbled to have played a small part in them turning their lives around.

Over all these years, *The Total Money Makeover* has given HOPE to millions of families. This book has given them hope to win, and that hope has caused them to take action and claim ultimate victory over their financial struggles and worries—and to actually *win*! The number of people I meet across this nation who tell me this is the first book of any kind they have read in ten years is staggering. *The Total Money Makeover* is a book for everyone. It is for high-income earners, as I am. And it is for someone beginning at the bottom, which is where I once was.

You are about to read about a process, a proven plan, to win. You will find the plan to be very simple yet very inspiring. The principles are not mine. I stole them all from God and your grandmother. The principles are common sense, which, again, isn't so common anymore. The plan is mine—and I'm no genius—created by simply observing millions of lives with whom I have interacted through radio, TV, books, classes, the Internet, email, podcasts, and our Live Events. I have successfully bottled common sense about money into a plan that anyone can do. And millions are!

When I first started talking about these principles years ago, I knew they had helped my wife, Sharon, and me survive going broke and begin to prosper. The first hundred times I spoke on money, I wasn't as confident of the principles as I am now. Nowadays I look into the eyes of a gazillion people who have followed this plan and experienced, as we did, excitement, hope, and gratitude. I am so thankful that I have not only given them a proven plan but have also inspired them to change their family tree.

I am so confident in *The Total Money Makeover* principles and this process that I cannot stand it when someone doesn't get it. Because I am so convinced my plan will work for everyone, my answers to the same questions will never change. By recognizing and identifying some basic truths and everyday common sense, I have convinced millions of people to change their lives—to have a Total Money Makeover. Are you next?

What This Book Is NOT

I know it may be hard for you to believe, but I get a lot of hate mail and criticism. This book and what I have or have not said in it have generated a lot of negativity and name-calling. That is fun. Not fun because I set out to offend or because I love reading the nasty things people often say. It is fun because the negativity means two things: one, for some people, we are touching a nerve that needs to be touched in order for them to change their lives, and two, I am actively and passionately pursuing the truth. Aristotle once said, "To avoid criticism say nothing, do nothing, and be nothing." I can't help millions of people change their lives by saying nothing, doing nothing, and being nothing. So I take the anger, the criticism, and even the hate mail as encouragement.

My publisher suggested I "answer my critics." I will pass. My grandmother used to say, "Those convinced against their will are of the same opinion still." However, I do not want you, dear reader, to be misled. So it is appropriate that I tell you what this book is NOT. That way you can decide whether or not to spend your hard-earned money on it.

This Book Is NOT Sophisticated or Complicated

If you are looking for a detailed, in-depth guide to investing, you have not found it. If you are looking for boring academic chirping that will put you to sleep using words only to support the author's ego, you have not found it. What I have discovered is that some of the most profound and life-changing truths you will ever discover are very simple.

In our culture we worship the complicated and the sophisticated. If you know what all the buttons on your remote control do, you may not have a good one. In the financial world we have been taught to be arrogant snobs. Some believe that simple ideas are not profound, that instead, simple ideas are for the "little people." That is a false and arrogant notion. I have met with thousands of millionaires, and in almost every case they keep their investing and money philosophies *very* uncomplicated. Just this week I was discussing investing and business structure with a friend of mine whose net worth is over twenty million dollars, and his words to me were, "I always keep it simple and clean." Only the financial goobers like to complicate things for the sake of justifying their existence or justifying how much they paid for their education. Please do not look here for a detailed guide to set up an estate plan or a deep theory on investing. That is not what I do. What I do is help people understand and act on time-honored truths about money that will truly change their whole lives.

This Book Is NOT Something That Has Never Been Said

There are many great money authors out there today, and there are even more in our past. Very little that you read in this book will be something that someone else has not written or said. We often say on our radio show that we give the same financial advice your grandmother would, only we keep our teeth in. I suggest you read a lot of different people, as I do. I have invented very little in this area of money. What I have done is packaged the time-honored information into a process that is doable and has inspired millions of people to act on it. Most of us know what to do; we just have trouble doing it. How do you lose weight? Exercise more and eat less. I know that, and yet I bought and read a couple of books on the subject while I took action, and I lost thirty pounds. Did the authors of those books tell me big ideas that were groundbreaking? No, they simply gave me an action plan and some supporting details to what I already knew had to be done. Welcome to my world.

This Book Is NOT Going to Mislead You on Investment Returns

There are several people in our country today who are ignorant on the returns offered by investing well. Ignorance is not lack of intelligence; it is simply "not knowing." Sadly, many intelligent but ignorant people seem to think that making a 12 percent rate of return on their money in a long-term investment is impossible. And that if I state that there is a 12 percent rate of return available, then I have lied to them or misled them.

I recommend good growth-stock mutual funds in this book as a long-term investment and dare to state that you should make 12 percent on your money over time. The supporting data for that bold statement can be found by looking at the historical averages of the Standard & Poor's 500 index. Widely regarded as the best single gauge of the US equities market, the S&P 500 is an index with five hundred of the largest companies in leading industries of the US economy. The S&P 500 has averaged 11.59 percent per year for the last ninety-plus years, as of this writing. This includes some pretty significant recession periods.

Does that mean you can expect to see 11–12 percent growth every year? Of course not. That's not how this thing works. The market goes up and down all the time, and sometimes it's a pretty wild ride. Just looking back over the past few years as of this writing, it looks like a roller coaster. In 2020, the market's annual return was 18.02 percent. In 2021, it was 28.47 percent. In 2022, it was actually down for the year at -18.01 percent.

But true long-term investors don't worry too much about the year-to-year returns. They look at the history over the long haul, knowing that some years it'll be up, and some years it'll be down.

Most experts and anyone who has had even one finance class agree that the S&P 500 is a great statistical measure of stock market returns. This is such a standard, or bellwether, that virtually every stock fund will show you its returns in comparison to the S&P 500. And again, the lifetime average of the S&P 500 is just under 12 percent. That's why I use it in my examples. It's not a magic number. It's just part of the conversation about investing.

I purchased a growth and income stock mutual fund many years ago that I still invest in, and it has averaged 12.03 percent per year since 1934, as of this writing. I bought another last week that has averaged over 13.9 percent per year since 1973, as of this writing. And yet another with average annual returns of 12.01 percent since 1984, and another averaging 12.39 percent since 1973, and yet another averaging 11.72 percent since 1952. Any decent broker with the heart of a teacher can, in his or her sleep, lead you to funds with long track records averaging over 12 percent. So don't let anyone tell you that you can't predict a 12 percent rate when you are considering investments for ten years or longer.

This Book Is NOT Just About Math, Statistics, Facts, and Figures

This book is about life. I've already said that personal finance is only 20 percent head knowledge. The other 80 percent—the bulk of the issue—is all about behavior. There's no magic number that will change your life, no interest rate or rate of return that will suddenly turn everything around. That's why I teach concepts, not mathematical formulas. The economic numbers, averages, and percentages may change over time, but the concepts and principles in this book won't.

This Book Is NOT Written by Someone with No Academic Credentials

I seldom list my formal academic credentials because, honestly, I don't think they are important. I have met so many broke people with financial credentials that I almost think it discredits me to have had formal training. Yes, I have a degree in finance. Yes, I have been or am licensed in real estate, insurance, and investments. Yes, I do have many of the stupid letters to put after my name. But the thing that qualifies me most to teach about money is that I have done stupid things with zeros on the end. I have been there, done that. I have a PhD in D-U-M-B. So I know what it is like to be scared and scarred. I know what it is like to have my marriage hanging by a thread because of financial stress. I know what it is like to have my hopes and dreams crushed by my own stupid decisions. *That* qualifies me uniquely to teach and to love hurting people. The other huge qualifier is that I used the principles I teach to personally build wealth. My wife and I have truly lived this book. The things we teach are not theory—they work!

But the teaching credentials that I am most sure of and which further qualify me are the hundreds of thousands of stories of people across America being set free by this book. This stuff simply works. So don't take financial advice from broke people.

This Book Is NOT Politically Correct

I stated earlier that personal finance is 80 percent behavior. To properly view behavior and to understand how to change behavior intelligently, we must consider several things. Behavior intelligently viewed takes into account the emotional, the relational, the family history, the socioeconomic impacts, and the spiritual. To ignore any of these while discussing behavior change about money is incomplete and very naive. So I openly discuss the spiritual in this book. As a Christian, I include some Bible verses. This is not a "Christian" book, and it for sure isn't a Bible study on the subject of money. But this is a book about a Proven Plan to Financial Peace that my team and I have developed over several decades, and that plan includes addressing the spiritual issues surrounding money. So I upset both sides—those who don't like it because I include spiritual thoughts in my teachings and those who don't believe my writing is spiritual enough. Either way, you have been warned.

This Book Is NOT Wrong

Don't confuse extreme confidence with arrogance. I am extremely confident that this material works because millions of people have benefited from it. I am not arrogant because I realize I am not personally responsible for any of the lives changed. The stuff I teach is the truth, and those principles are responsible for changing lives. But I always answer the same questions with the same answers even though sometimes folks think their situation may be different. It isn't different. The principles stand, and they work every time.

This Book Is NOT the Same as My Other Books

When we took on *The Total Money Makeover* project, we had to answer a question of integrity: Could we honestly go into the market and ask my readers to buy another book that said the same thing? I couldn't in good conscience do that. *Financial Peace* has sold millions of copies as of this writing, so did I really need to write another book? I came to the conclusion that there was a distinct difference in the two projects. *Financial Peace* is "what to do with money." It is a great textbook for common-sense money management. So how is *The Total Money Makeover* different? It is more than a "what to do" book—it is a "how to do it" plan. This is a process book. We are aiming at carefully weaving inspiration and information together into a step-by-step plan. Yes, you will find in this book a lot of the same subjects, along with many of the same principles I discuss in my other books, but this book is different in that it is a process-driven work.

If you are looking for a ton of new information because you are someone who only gathers facts and figures, then you will be disappointed. If you are looking to engage this money thing head-on, you will love this book. Many *Financial Peace* readers have told me that *The Total Money Makeover* gave legs to the concepts to which they had been introduced, so they were thankful to read it as well. But again, don't look for some big revelation or chapters of new principles.

This Book Is **NOT** Getting Any Complaints or Criticism . . .

. . . from people who do it. I have never had someone write to me, saying, "I got on a budget, got out of debt, got on the same page with my spouse, built wealth—and I HATE IT." For those who have followed this plan and discovered a new life of financial freedom, their lives have been changed *forever*! Wouldn't you like to experience the same transformation? You can be the next success story people hear about. You can have a Total Money Makeover starting today!

Flying Turkeys and Skinny-Dipping

When I was a child, my grandmother—a second-grade schoolteacher who also taught drama—used to sit me on her knee and read to me. She read with great enthusiasm and a *lot* of drama.

One of the children's stories she read to me was about the three little pigs. One built his house out of straw, one out of twigs, and one out of brick. You know the story—the two who built their houses "quick and dirty" goofed off, partied, and made fun of the bricklayer because he was taking too much time and effort to do it *right*. Of course, when the wind and rains came, the two short-term thinkers ended up moving in with their brother. Why? Because he had prepared well enough to weather the storms. The other two found their lives completely blown apart.

The Good News and Bad News About Economic Storms

If you are reading this and you are over the age of 25, you have already endured several significant economic storms. You have seen the Dot-Com Crash and the economic fallout from the terror attacks of 9/11. You have been witness to high-profile corporate scandals and huge stock market losses. You have survived the Great Recession that led to 10 percent unemployment, record numbers of foreclosures, and the gutting of retirement accounts for millions of Americans. And, as if we could forget (if only we could forget), there was the COVID-19 recession, a steep but thankfully short-lived recession sparked by lockdowns, closings, and an inevitable decline in consumer activity. These are real economic storms with real consequences for real people. And they are just the tip of the iceberg. The U.S. has powered through more than a dozen recessions, rising (and falling) interest rates, inflation, stock market twists and turns, wars, and conflicts since World War II.

The good news about economic storms like these is that we do recover. Some of us learn painful lessons on a private, individual level; others learn the economic lessons on a more widespread, national level. Many people don't learn anything at all.

The great news is that, for some, events like these can become your Great Depression, emotionally speaking. The Great Depression permanently changed the way many people of that generation handled their money. If you are fortunate enough to know someone who was an adult during that time, he or she likely has a completely different way of looking at debt, saving, and giving than most people of other generations. That is because they had an experience. And as my pastor says, "A man with an experience is not at the mercy of a man with an opinion."

I went broke in my late twenties, and that experience changed my life. It even changed how outside economic turmoil affected me. Take the Great Recession, for example. By the time it hit in 2008, I had already been applying the principles of this book to my life for two and a half decades before, so I was just a spectator. It didn't hurt me a bit. I actually came out ahead by buying real estate at great prices and investing heavily in the stock market while both were down.

I've spent the last thirty years trying to get people to live these Total Money Makeover principles. Those who listened are just as ready as I am for the next time the winds blow and the storms come. They have a strong foundation.

Flying Turkeys

What does all this mean for your Total Money Makeover? The first lesson of this economic storm is that your financial process and principles must work in good times *and* in bad times—otherwise, they don't work. An interesting fact about modern economic cycles is that the average period of recession lasts about ten months while the average period of economic growth is nearly six times longer—57 months. When the economy is booming for that long, really stupid ideas start to look like they work in the short term. That fools people into believing that stupid is smart. But when stupid finally gets stress tested, it comes up looking, well, stupid.

When times are booming, you can do dumb things with money, get sloppy, and take huge risks without realizing it. I have heard it said this way: "Even a turkey can fly in a tornado." People run around buying things they can't afford with money they don't have to impress people they don't even like, and they do it in record numbers. Worse, they seem to get away with it!

They're like the two little pigs with straw and twig homes: As long as the sun is shining, life is a party, and the pig with brick seems kind of nerdy, or overly conservative, or even fanatical. But when their stupid theories are stress tested, their houses fall.

Jim Collins, one of America's greatest business writers, wrote a book called *How the Mighty Fall*. In this book, he discusses the five stages of decline when a business fails, or falls. There is a great application here for our nation's economy and for *your* life and mine.

Collins says the first stage of decline is marked by hubris. Pride and arrogance, mixed with a false notion of invincibility, lead the mighty to take huge, ridiculous risks. In our case, that would be borrowing lots of money and not saving any because "my job is 'stable.' I can afford the 'easy payments' with my 'job.'"

This hubris causes sloppiness and denial of risk. Hey, that sounds like me in my late twenties—right before I went broke. I had been taught a group of myths—*lies*—that I accepted as truth about money. I thought the rules of risk and restraint didn't apply to me because I was so smart. That led me to build a house of cards that fell the first time there was a light breeze, much less a real storm.

Here's the lesson: Just because you see a turkey flying in a tornado doesn't mean turkeys can fly. Just because some wild-eyed theory of investing, borrowing, and living without cash reserves works in good times doesn't mean you can survive a storm. Remember, your ways of handling money have to work in good times *and* in bad.

Skinny-Dipping

Warren Buffett has a great saying: "When the tide goes out, you can tell who was skinny-dipping." I have taught for years that if you have a bad map, you will be late for—or completely miss—the party. The principles that you build your life on will determine your level of success. If you plan your marriage around a bad map, or bad set of assumptions, then it will likely fail. If you have all the good intentions in the world but build your financial house on bad ideas, it will fall. I personally experienced this a long time ago. With each recession or bubble, many more Americans discover that their theories about money and their assumptions about how money works are wrong. And they discover they are wrong the hard way—through pain.

Overspending that doesn't *feel* like overspending because things are going well is *still* overspending. Using debt to invest in real estate or the stock market with the hope of a quick return will cause you to go broke the minute the market turns. Chasing the next get-rich-quick scam, like the lottery or investing in cryptocurrencies or, heaven help us, NFTs, will always bring you pain. Hiring someone else—like some debt-settlement company—to fix your life virtually never works.

The myths—*lies* spread by our culture—that were covered in this book's first three editions have *all* been proven by the economic storms we've encountered. If you live the way we teach in this book, you will prosper in good times *and* in bad times.

I have a friend whom we will call Chris. Chris told me an interesting story in the middle of the Great Recession that illustrates what I am pointing out to you. For thirteen years, Chris worked for a large corporation whose name you would recognize. He started his Total Money Makeover a few years before the recession began. When I saw him five years later, he ran up to me with a big smile and big hug to proudly proclaim that he was "DEBT FREE!!" including his home. He had absolutely no debt and had saved $38,000 in his emergency fund.

When I saw him again a year later, he had another fun story to share with me. It seems that he and his boss had become best friends over the years that they worked together. That week his friend—his boss—came into his office, with blood drained from his face and his lip quivering, saying, "I don't know how to tell you this, but corporate is making me lay you off." Chris jumped up from his chair, ran around the desk, gave his friend a big hug, and said, "Cool! How much is the severance?"

The company gave him more than $70,000 in severance, which he used to start his own business—something he had wanted to do for years. He wasn't stressed, but instead saw only opportunity, because he was ready. It wasn't long until he made almost double his old salary with his new business. Wow.

However, most people live on the other side of the coin. When they get news of a layoff, they have the blood drain from their faces and it is their lips that are quivering. If you have lost your job and are struggling, I am not picking on you. I have seen hard times. But I want you to do what I did when I faced pain brought on by my own stupid decisions and lack of preparation. I said very loudly, "NEVER AGAIN!" Next time . . . well, there won't be a next time.

That doesn't mean there won't be another economic storm to endure. My faith in our government to screw things up is strong enough for me to guarantee you will see many more recessions, bear markets, and inflationary spirals in your lifetime. In fact, there will always be some big-picture economic chaos going on. And there's nothing you or I can do to control that. The whole point of your Total Money Makeover is for you to learn to control the things you can control. What can you control? Your habits, your choices, and your actions. When you build good money habits like budgeting and living on less than you make, when you choose to stop doing what broke people do and start doing what rich people do, you can win no matter what is happening with the economy. What are you waiting for? It is time for your Total Money Makeover. Are you ready?

The Total Money Makeover Challenge

"As lost as a ball in tall weeds!" That is exactly how I felt. Although it was decades ago, I can still taste the emotion as if it were yesterday. Out of control, lost, no sense of power, I felt dread creep across the room like the afternoon shadows on a cold winter's day. Sitting again at the kitchen table with too much month left at the end of the money, I was not having fun. This "adult" stuff where a wife looks to you to provide and kids expect to be fed and kept warm was not exactly working. I didn't feel like some powerful adult; instead, there was a little boy inside me who was very afraid—afraid of this month's bills, afraid of this month's mortgage, and absolutely terrified when I considered the future. How was I to send kids to college, retire, enjoy life, and not live at the edge of money worries?

The "Normal" American Family

It seemed every month I sat at that same table with the same worries, fears, and problems. I had too much debt, too little savings, and no sense of control over my life. No matter how hard I worked, it seemed I couldn't win. I was to forever be a slave to some banker, to the government, and to the "needs" of my family. When Sharon and I "talked" about money, we ended up in a fight, leaving her feeling afraid and me feeling inadequate. The next car purchase, the next house, the kids' college—our entire future seemed out of reach.

I didn't need a get-rich-quick guy to pump me up or tell me to be positive. I didn't need a secret formula to riches. I wasn't afraid of hard work or sacrifice. I didn't want to "feel" my way into being "positive." I was positive of only one thing: I was sick and tired of being sick and tired. I was tired of sitting down to "do the bills" and having a heaviness come over me. The hopelessness was overwhelming. I felt like a gerbil in a wheel—run, run, run, no traction, no ground covered; maybe life was just a financial illusion. All the money came in, all the money went out, and only the names were changed to protect the innocent. I owe, I owe, so off to work I go. You know the drill and all the clichés that go with the drill.

Oh, some months everything seemed to work, and I thought maybe we were going to be okay. I could tell myself then, "Oh well, this is how everyone lives." Those times offered enough wiggle room that I could continue to lie to myself that we were making headway, but deep down, I knew we weren't.

I Did It My Way, and My Way Wasn't Working

ENOUGH! THIS STINKS! I finally decided that this nonplan wasn't working. If you have ever had any of those feelings, you are going to love this book, and, more important, you will love your Total Money Makeover.

Back in our late twenties, my wife, Sharon, and I went broke. We lost everything due to my stupidity in handling money, or not handling it, as the case may be. Hitting bottom and hitting it hard was the worst thing that ever happened to me and the best thing that ever happened to me.

We started with nothing, but by the time I was twenty-six years old, we held real estate worth over $4 million. I was good at real estate, but I was better at borrowing money. Even though I had become a millionaire, I had built a house of cards. The short version of the story is that we went through financial hell and lost everything over a three-year period of time. We were sued, foreclosed on, and, finally, with a brand-new baby and a toddler, we were bankrupt. *Scared* doesn't begin to cover it. *Crushed* comes close, but we held on to each other and decided we needed a change.

So after losing everything, I went on a quest, a quest to find out how money really works, how I could get control of it, and how I could have confidence in handling it. I read everything I could get my hands on. I interviewed older rich people, people who made money and kept it. That quest led me to a really, really uncomfortable place—my mirror. I came to realize that my money problems, worries, and shortages largely began and ended with the person in my mirror. I realized also that if I could learn to manage the character I shaved with every morning, I could win at money. That quest, the one that ended with me staring at myself in the mirror, led me on a new journey: the journey of helping others, literally millions of others, take that same quest to the mirror. Live Events, *Financial Peace University*, *The Ramsey Show*, and the national bestsellers *Financial Peace*, *More Than Enough*, *The Total Money Makeover*, *EntreLeadership,* and *Baby Steps Millionaires* have enabled me to tell millions of Americans what I have learned—the hard way—about money.

The Big Challenge: Find a Mirror

I have a challenge for you. Are you ready to take on the guy or gal in your mirror? If you are, you are ready to win. I rediscovered God's and Grandma's simple way of handling money. Wealth building isn't rocket science, which is a good thing for me (and probably you). Winning at money is 80 percent behavior and 20 percent head knowledge. What to do isn't the problem; doing it is. Most of us know what to do, but we just don't do it. If I can control the guy in the mirror, I can be skinny and rich.

We will let other books work on the skinny, and I will help you with the rich part. No, there are no secrets, and yes, this will be very hard. Hey, if it were easy, every moron walking would be wealthy.

So my Total Money Makeover begins with a challenge. The challenge is you. You are the problem with your money. The financial channel or some late-night infomercial gimmick aren't your answer; you are. You are the king of your future, and I have a plan. The Total Money Makeover plan isn't theory. It works every single time. It works because it is simple. It works because it gets to the heart of your money problems: you. It is based on a series of prices that must be paid to win. All winners pay a price to win. Some losers pay a price and never win, and that is usually because they didn't have the benefit of a proven plan for financial fitness.

Ordinary People

Tens of thousands of ordinary people have used the system in this book to get out of debt, regain control, and build wealth. I've scattered their stories throughout the book. If at any point during your makeover you are tempted to quit or you just need a little encouragement, read one of these stories. These people have sacrificed for a short period of time so they will never have to sacrifice again.

If you are looking for a road map to get you home, you've found it. If you are looking for something easy or fast, you have the wrong book. If you are looking for a book to help you pass your CPA exam in the area of financial knowledge, you have the wrong book. If you are looking for a writer who has intricate academic theories (that don't work in the real world), you've got the wrong guy. I have many of the academic pedigrees, but I ended up broke. I have actually twice become a millionaire from nothing. The first time I was in my twenties, the money was in real estate, and I lost that due to my stupidity; the second time I was not yet forty, but I did the money thing right that time, and I am debt-free.

I often hear about broke finance professors who bemoan that I am way too simple, or as an emailer told me on *The Ramsey Show* one day, "You are a one-trick pony." To those of you who say you have great but unexecuted plans, I say, "Prove it. I have." I like the way I've built wealth better than the way you haven't. You will meet people, educated and uneducated, throughout this book who have won, or begun to win, with money for the first time in their lives. The Total Money Makeover works!

The Total Money Makeover Motto

This plan works, but it will cost you. It will teach you to say new words, like *no*. In short, your Total Money Makeover will be a personal money makeover where you learn this motto: IF YOU WILL LIVE LIKE NO ONE ELSE, LATER YOU CAN LIVE LIKE NO ONE ELSE. This is the motto of your Total Money Makeover. It's my way of reminding you that if you will make the sacrifices now that most people aren't willing to make, later on you will be able to live as those folks will never be able to live. You will notice the motto all through the book, even across the bottom of the pages. I'm sorry there isn't an easier path to feature in the motto, but the good thing about this one is that it works. You can repeat the motto to yourself as you pass up a purchase in order to hit your goals. When you work late and are tired, you can say the motto to yourself. Of course, this isn't a magic formula; I'm not into that. But it does remind you that you *will* win, and the payoff *will* be worth the cost.

Some of you are so immature that you are unwilling to delay pleasure for a greater result. I will show you exactly how to get the result you want, so the price you pay will not be in vain. I don't want to walk across hot coals because it is fun, but if I can be shown how a short, painful walk will do away with the lifetime of worry, frustration, stress, and fear that being constantly broke brings me, then bring on the hot coals.

Early on in our marriage, we decided that Kari would stay home with our children rather than working outside the home. This decision has perhaps disadvantaged us financially at times, but it has been the best choice for our family in many other regards.

Financially, we have made some mistakes, such as keeping our student loans around because of the "low interest" and even leasing a car at one point. To us, credit cards were a status symbol, and we had a few. Our debt peaked at about $375,000 (including the mortgage). That's not the smartest situation to get yourself into when you have four kids and one salary. By the time we got on Dave's plan, we were ready to work with gazelle intensity to get rid of our debt! During one six-month period we paid off $57,000 and gave $7,000 to our church. That really encouraged us and kept us going! It was also great going to Atlantis with Dave and Sharon as finalists in The Total Money Makeover Challenge!

Now we are debt-free and helping our daughter through her first year of college. We are also saving for retirement at a good rate and building a new house. We enjoy earning interest now, rather than paying it. We couldn't have done it without Dave. We pay cash for everything, and we tell our money where to go. We can't even tell you the peace and freedom this has brought our entire family!

The first months were the most painful as we went from credit to cash. But it's so nice not to be paying for today and yesterday anymore! By following Dave's Total Money Makeover plan, you will gain peace of mind as you get control of your money. Just remember to stay focused.

The key to our success was both of us getting on the same page at the same time. We now work together to plan our spending rather than racing to outspend each other. We are each other's source of strength during weak moments when spending sounds fun again. We have learned to have FUN talking about money and financial goals. It's no longer a contentious subject.

Our advice: Honestly assess your earning capacity and live below your means. Be in control of your own destiny and your own happiness!

**Mark and
Kari Stolworthy (both age 43)**
*CPA/Systems Consultant;
Stay-at-Home Mom*

My Promise to You

My promise to you is this: If you will follow the guidelines of this proven system of sacrifice and discipline, you can be debt-free, begin saving, and give as you've never given before. You will build wealth. I will also promise you that it is totally up to you. The Total Money Makeover isn't a magic formula to wealth. This system will not work unless you do, and then only to the degree of your intensity in implementing it. In the following pages, you will meet many individuals and families who have won many money victories, but not one of them won until they won the battle with the guy in the mirror. Your situation isn't your spouse's fault (well, maybe, but we'll talk later), it isn't your parents' fault, it isn't your children's fault, and it isn't your friends' fault. IT IS YOUR FAULT!

But guess what? That means that if you're the one who got you into this mess, you're the one who can get you out. No law, regulation, or mandate will fix you. No politician's promises or government handout will fix you. No dream job or sky-high salary will fix you. Some of those things may help, but none of them will do a thing unless you take charge of your own life. This is your life, your call, your future. This is 100 percent your decision. If you're ready to move, then let's get going. Right now. I'll lead the way. But I won't push you across the starting line, and I can't drag you across the finish line. This whole journey from start to finish is up to you.

My financial life began turning around when I took responsibility for it. People all across America have used these steps to become free, regain

> ### DAVE RANTS . . .
>
> Savings without a mission is garbage. Your money needs to work for you, not lie around you.

a sense of confidence and control, and build a future for their families. Please join me on a journey away from the young man I was, the one I described earlier who was racked with worry, fear, and guilt over money. Take this journey with me to your own Total Money Makeover, but remember, the first part of the quest is confronting the man in the mirror. That man in the mirror is your Total Money Makeover Challenge.

2

Denial: I'm Not *That* Out of Shape

Several years ago I realized I had let my body dissolve into flab. I had worked so hard for so many years that I had abandoned the care of my physical condition. The first step to getting into shape was to realize I needed to change my ways, but the second and equally important step was to identify the obstacles to getting there. What would stop me from getting into shape? Once I understood those obstacles, I began a process to lose weight, grow muscle, and become fitter. Your Total Money Makeover is the same. You need to realize there's a problem, but you must also see what could hinder your move toward financial fitness. The next few chapters will identify some major obstacles to YOUR Total Money Makeover.

Look in the mirror. Take a long look. What do you see? Suck in that gut; hold up your chest, and really look at yourself. It doesn't matter how many angles or poses you take; the mirror is cruel. "Well, I'm really not *that* fat, maybe just a little flabby." My dad used to say that 90 percent of solving a problem is realizing there is one. Focused intensity, life-or-death intensity, is required for you to reset your money-spending patterns, and one of your biggest obstacles is DENIAL. The sad thing is that you can be financially mediocre in this country, financially flabby, and still be

9

average. And if the truth be known, being average, normal, and financially flabby is pretty much okay by most folks' standards. This, however, is not a book for the wimpy among us. This is a book about winning, about really having something.

We started out our marriage with absolutely no debt. We lived on a single income, the cars were paid for, and we even had a small amount of savings. However, we eventually made the misguided decision to move into a much larger house that stretched us financially. After a few years, I changed jobs and we increased our annual income—giving us the illusion that we could increase our standard of living. That is when the debt really started accumulating. We financed two NEW cars to replace our old ones. We started buying everything on credit. We even got a home equity loan. Before we realized it, we were buried in debt!

Kelley saw *The Total Money Makeover* in our local bookstore and bought it as a Father's Day gift for me. By Independence Day, we had declared war on our debt! We had $6,000 in savings but $16,000 in debt, not including our house. The plan required us to take out $5,000 from our savings to put toward our debt—leaving us with the $1,000 Baby emergency fund. It was tough seeing our hard-earned savings disappear, but it really helped our debt snowball get rolling. We sacrificed in other areas, and in just ten months we paid off all of our consumer debt!

Dave helped us realize that we had to draw the line and stop living beyond our means. Instead of having to pay our creditors each month, we can finally start paying ourselves and investing in our future!

Mark (age 40) and
Kelley (age 39) Reep
Civil Engineer; Nursing School Student

Don't Wait to Have Denial Knocked Out of You

I regularly speak to live audiences of two to twelve thousand people, teaching them the ideas in this book. After one Live Event where I spoke to four thousand people, Sara told me that her Total Money Makeover came only after life placed a call to her. She said she had heard me quote the *Wall Street Journal* as reporting that 70 percent of Americans live paycheck to paycheck, but she honestly thought she was in the 30 percent who were fine. She had financially struck a pose, and the pose was denial.

With two sons from her previous marriage, Sara had just remarried and was happy and secure in her job, as was her husband, John. Their new life together seemed awesome. Their household combined income was about $75,000 per year, with the "normal" debts of a small student loan, a car loan, and "only" $5,000 on a credit card. With life under control and even going well, Sara and John decided their new family needed a new home, so the builder was selected and construction began. Somewhere deep inside there may have been uneasiness, but it was very deep. Finally, the day came when the new home was complete. Everything was going to be fine now, the new family in the new home, the way it is "supposed" to be. In May, they moved into the new home, complete with big new payments.

In September, Sara's boss asked to see her in his office. She was excelling at work and braced herself for a big "attagirl" followed by a nice bonus or raise. Instead, the boss explained her job was being eliminated. "Downsizing, you know," he said. Her life's work was cut from her—and $45,000 of their $75,000 income—with the boss's chilling words. Not only was her pride hurt and her career path cut short but a creeping terror grew deep down inside as she drove home to tell John. That night there were tears, fears, and the sudden stark realization that she and John were financially fat. Suddenly, Sara and her family were facing foreclosure on the house and repossession of the car. The basics of life had become precious.

Sara and John had listened to *The Ramsey Show* on the radio, but they always thought someone else needed a Total Money Makeover. After all, they always held their stomachs in when standing in front of the mirror. The night after her layoff was the first night they looked in the financial mirror and saw fat people. The sight wasn't pretty—big house payments, fat car payments, large student loans, bloated credit cards, anorexic savings, and no budget. They saw fat people.

When you are physically fat, it is hard to be in denial, because there is the ever-widening belt line. When you are financially fat, however, you can fake it and look good for a while. Your friends and family will participate in your fantasy/denial, which makes you believe you are doing just fine.

> **DAVE RANTS...**
>
> For your own good, for the good of your family and your future, grow a backbone. When something is wrong, stand up and say it is wrong, and don't back down.

One of the four major factors that keep people from winning in money by getting a Total Money Makeover is not realizing they need one. Sadly, some of the most dramatic makeovers I've seen have been by people who had life smack them so hard they got the denial knocked out of them, like Sara. If life isn't smacking you around at the moment, you are actually in greater danger than Sara and John the night of the layoff. You are a real candidate for financial mediocrity or even a major crisis brought on by denial, and you have to see the need to make dramatic changes. If you are apathetic because everything seems "just fine," then you will be unwilling to make the huge changes needed to get huge results.

Mmm . . . Frog Legs

Years ago, in a motivational seminar by the master, Zig Ziglar, I heard a story about how mediocrity will sneak up on you. The story goes that if you drop a frog into boiling water, he will sense the pain and immediately jump out. However, if you put a frog in room-temperature water, he will swim around happily, and as you gradually turn the water up to boiling, the frog will not sense the change. The frog is lured to his death by gradual change. We can lose our health, our fitness, and our wealth gradually, one day at a time. It might be a cliché, but that's because it is true: The enemy of "the best" is not "the worst." The enemy of "the best" is "just fine."

I was in denial for a long time about my life and my spending habits. By my mid-twenties, I was $23,000 in debt and had little motivation to get out of it. My biggest problem wasn't realizing how nice it was to be free of financial concerns—it was gambling. I couldn't stop. Even when I began listening to *The Ramsey Show* and tried to start attacking my debt, I often failed. I kept losing my money to the addiction I had—never giving me time to get my feet on the ground.

It took some time, but finally the financial pressures became too much to bear. I knew I needed a change. I started attending an amazing program called Celebrate Recovery, a ministry dedicated to helping people with addictions, hurts, and hang-ups.

I also started my Total Money Makeover walking through the Baby Steps one by one. Establishing my emergency fund was the hardest part because I was still trying to break my gambling addiction, and that money would always get lost to some game. But as my addiction weakened and I established a budget, the debt I had incurred became less and less. I moved in with my parents to put would-be rent money toward my final debt.

Now I'm saving for a down payment on a house. I hope to reach my goal by next year. It is a wonderful feeling to live without the strain of debt on my life!

Tony E. Newman (age 26)
Financial Analyst

The Pain of Change

Change is painful. Few people have the courage to seek out change. Most people won't change until the pain of where they are exceeds the pain of change. When it comes to money, we can be like the toddler in a soiled diaper. "I know it smells bad, but it's warm and it's mine." Only when the rash comes will we cry out. I hope Sara's story and the others in this book will make you unwilling to stay where you are. If you keep doing the same things, you will keep getting the same results. You are where you are right now financially as a sum total of the decisions you've made to this point. If you like where you are, keep it up. Keep in mind, however, why you are reading a book called *The Total Money Makeover*. Is it because deep down you have the same uneasy feeling Sara had but didn't address until it was almost too late? Are you really looking for something more? If so, I've got great news. This plan works! Break through the temptation to remain in the same situation, and opt for the pain of change before the pain of not changing searches you out. Don't wait for a heart attack to show you that you are overweight. Cut the carbs, the fats, and the sugars, and lace up the running shoes now.

The good news about Sara and John was that the financial heart attack they had made them address their financial eating and exercise habits. The layoff was a wake-up call and the end to denial. After a year of very hard times, Sara was able to find a whole new career. Only this time when the checks started rolling in, Sara and John were using this system. Every paycheck became an exciting event because they had a plan. They were financially losing weight and toning up. It wasn't a quick process, but after following the steps over time, today they are really winning.

The night I met Sara and John, they were two years into their plan—and smiling. They told me they were debt-free except for their house, and they had $12,000 in the bank just for emergencies. They had broken through their own denial, but they made their family uncomfortable because they refused to live like everyone else. Albert Einstein said, "Great spirits have often encountered violent opposition from weak minds." John's dad had made fun of their plan and the extra jobs they took to win. He asked if they had joined some cult or something. Once Sara and John had realized they were the emperor with no clothes, denial was no longer an option. They also realized all they had been doing with money to impress others—but no more.

Sara chuckled as she told me how she used to think: *We must be doing well; all these credit card companies think I'm creditworthy. If I'm getting approvals from all these banks, I must be okay because, otherwise, they wouldn't want to loan me money. Besides, I pay my credit cards off every month. How could I be in any trouble? I can afford to buy that car or that furniture if I can afford the payment.* John was grinning now, too, as they both laughed at the language of financially fat people who think they are fine, the language of denial.

As we closed our conversation that night, Sara told me that while she hoped she or John never lost another job unexpectedly, they are ready if they do. "We are no longer living a lie. We know where we are, we know where we are going, and we know how we are going to get there," she said. She and John wanted to leave me a gift for inspiring their Total Money Makeover, but I assured them they already had.

EveryDollar helps you plan your monthly cash flow so you always know where you are with your money. Scan the QR code to get started.

3

Debt Myths: Debt Is (Not) a Tool

Red-faced and fists clenched, the toddler yells with murder in his voice, "I want it! I want it! I want it!" We have all watched this scene unfold in the grocery store. We may even have watched our own children do this (once). Now that I'm older and more mellow, I sometimes grin a little as a young mom tries without success to stifle the out-of-control screams of a child who is denied something.

It is human nature to want it and want it now; it is also a sign of immaturity. Being willing to delay pleasure for a greater result is a sign of maturity. However, our culture teaches us to live for the now. "I want it!" we scream, and we can get it if we are willing to go into debt. Debt is a means to obtain the "I want its" before we can afford them.

Joining in the Lie

I have heard it said that if you tell a lie often enough, loudly enough, and long enough, the myth will become accepted as a fact. Repetition, volume, and longevity will twist and turn a myth, or a lie, into a commonly accepted way of doing things. Entire populations have been lulled into the approval of ghastly deeds and even participation in them by gradually moving from

16

the truth to a lie. Throughout history, twisted logic, rationalization, and incremental changes have allowed normally intelligent people to be party to ridiculous things. Propaganda, in particular, has played a big part in allowing these things to happen.

We have propaganda in our culture today. I'm not speaking in a political sense, but rather recognizing that there are people out there who want us to think their way, and who will go to great lengths to accomplish that. The financial and banking industries, in particular, are very good at teaching us their way of handling money, which, of course, leads us to buy their products. If I see an ad again and again that tells me I will be cool and sharp-looking if I drive a certain car, I can fall under the illusion that with the purchase of that car, those good things will happen to me. We may not really believe that we will become a model just from purchasing a car, but notice that ugly people aren't used in the TV spots to sell cars. We aren't really falling for that lie—or are we? I'm just asking. After all, we do buy the car and then justify our purchase on the basis of something academic like gas mileage.

When we participate in what the crowd identifies as normal, even if it is stupid, we gain acceptance into the club. Sometimes we don't even realize what we are doing is stupid because we have been taught that it's just "the way you do it," and so we never ask why. As we participate in the myth, we learn to spout the principles of the myth. After the years go by and we have invested more money and time into the myth, we become great disciples and can preach the points of the myth with great fervor and volume. We become such experts on the myth that we can sell others on joining the lie. I once joined in the lie, but no more.

Don't Let the Monkeys Pull You Down!

Debt has been sold to us so aggressively, so loudly, and so often that to imagine living without debt requires myth-busting. We have to systematically destroy the inner workings of the myths. Debt is so ingrained into our culture that most Americans cannot even envision a car without a payment, a house without a mortgage, a student without a loan, and a card without credit. We have been sold debt with such repetition and with such fervor that most folks cannot conceive what it would be like to have no payments. Just as slaves born into slavery can't visualize freedom, we Americans don't know what it would be like to wake up to no debt. Literally billions of credit card offers hit our mailboxes and inboxes every year, and we are taking advantage of those offers. Americans currently have more than $1 trillion in credit card debt. We can't do without debt—or can we?

Working with tens of thousands of people on their Total Money Makeovers over the years, I have found that a major barrier to winning is our view of debt. Most people who have made the decision to stop borrowing money have experienced something weird: ridicule. Friends and family who are disciples of the myth that debt is good have ridiculed those on the path to freedom.

John Maxwell tells of a study done on monkeys. A group of monkeys were locked in a room with a pole at the center. Some luscious, ripe bananas were placed on top of the pole. When a monkey would begin to climb the pole, the experimenters would knock him off with a blast of water from a fire hose. Each time a monkey would climb, off he would go, until all the monkeys had been knocked off repeatedly, thus learning that the climb was hopeless. The experimenters then observed that the other primates would pull down any monkey trying to climb. They replaced a single monkey with one who didn't know the system. As soon as the new guy tried to climb, the others would pull him down and punish him for trying. One by one, each monkey was replaced, and the scene repeated until there were no monkeys left in the room that had experienced the fire hose. Still, none of the new guys were allowed to climb. The other monkeys pulled them down. Not one monkey in the room knew why, but none were allowed to get the bananas.

We aren't monkeys, but sometimes we exhibit behavior that seems rather chimp-like. We don't even remember why; we just know that debt is needed to win. So when a loved one decides to get a Total Money Makeover, we laugh, get angry, and pull him down. We Americans are like the last set of monkeys. With rolled eyes we spout the pat lines associated with the myth as if anyone not wanting to have debt is unintelligent. That person must be a simpleton, a fanatic, or, worst of all, "uneducated in finance." Then why are so many finance professors broke? I think a broke finance professor is like a shop teacher with missing fingers.

Myth vs. Truth

I want to expose the inner workings of the Debt Myth by looking at many of the sub-myths. However, I need to warn you to watch out for your instinct to defend the American way of borrowing. Calm down. Relax and go for a ride with me for a few pages. I might be on to something. If, at the end of this myth-busting section, you conclude I'm just a nut with a book, you will not be forced to change. But just in case the tens of thousands of families who have experienced a Total Money Makeover have something to say to you, read on in a relaxed state. Let your guard down. You can always put the shields back up later.

MYTH: Debt is a tool and should be used to create prosperity.

TRUTH: Debt adds considerable risk, most often doesn't bring prosperity, and isn't used by wealthy people nearly as much as we are led to believe.

When training for my first career in real estate, I remember being told that debt was a tool. "Debt is like a fulcrum and lever," allowing us to lift what we otherwise could not. We can buy a home, a car, start a business, or go out to eat and not be bothered with having to wait. I remember a finance professor telling us that debt was a two-edged sword, which could cut for you like a tool but could also cut into you and bring harm. The myth has been sold that we should use OPM, other people's money, to prosper. The academic garbage is spread really thick on this issue. We are told with sufficient snobbery and noses in the air that sophisticated and disciplined financiers use debt to their advantage. Careful there, you'll get a sunburn on your upper lip.

My contention is that debt brings on enough risk to offset any advantage that could be gained through leverage of debt. Given time, a lifetime, risk will destroy the perceived returns purported by the mythsayers.

I once was a mythsayer myself and could repeat the myths very convincingly. I was especially good with the "debt is a tool" myth. I have even sold rental property that was losing money to investors by showing them, with very sophisticated internal rates of return, how they would actually make money. Boy, what a reach. I could spout the myth with enthusiasm, but life and God had some lessons to teach me. Only after losing everything I owned and finding myself bankrupt did I think that risk should be factored in, even mathematically. It took my waking up in "intensive care" to realize how dumb and dangerous this myth is. Life hit me hard enough to get my attention and teach me. According to Proverbs 22:7: "The rich rule over the poor, and the borrower is slave to the lender" (NIV). I was confronted with this scripture and had to make a conscious decision of who was right—my broke finance professor, who taught that debt is a tool, or God, who showed obvious disdain for debt. Beverly Sills had it right when she said, "There is no shortcut to anyplace worth going."

We bought the lie! We lived our lives according to the standards set to "keep up with the Joneses." Turns out they were broke and living in debt too. My husband and I owed $72,000 on a rental property and $35,000 on credit cards, student loans, and car notes. And on top of that, we bought a four-bedroom home complete with a pool that was in need of major repairs—all of this on a $40,000 teacher's salary. But we decided that all of this was a good investment in our future. We were so wrong!

We were sick and tired of always having more month than money. We needed a Total Money Makeover. We sold our rental property and our WAY-too-big house and downsized to something much smaller. We spent two and a half years of focused intensity to finally become DEBT-FREE!

If you are living in the bondage of debt, you're not living. Our marriage is so much better, and there is an element of peace that wasn't there before we had a financial plan. We feel blessed to have found this information early in our marriage and thankful to have the opportunity to teach our children to be financially responsible.

**Alison (age 29) and
Mike (age 33) Wessner**
*Homemaker; Physical Education
Teacher*

I have found that if you look into the lives of the kind of people you want to be like, you will find common themes. If you want to be skinny, study skinny people, and if you want to be rich, do what lots of rich people do, not what some mythsayer says to do. The Forbes 400 is a list of the richest four hundred people in America as rated by *Forbes* magazine. When surveyed, 75 percent of the Forbes 400 (rich people, not your broke brother-in-law with an opinion) said the best way to build wealth is to become and stay debt-free. Chick-Fil-A, Hobby Lobby, and Intuitive Surgical, Inc. are run debt-free. I have met with thousands of millionaires in my years as a financial counselor, and I have never met one who said he made it all with Discover Card bonus points. They all lived on less than they made and spent only when they had cash. No payments.

History also teaches us that debt wasn't always a way of life; in fact, three of the biggest lenders of the last century were founded by people who hated debt. Before it filed for bankruptcy, Sears was a powerful force in retail and made more money on credit than on the sale of merchandise. They weren't really a store; they were a lender with some stuff out front (makes you wonder why they went bankrupt, right?). However, in 1910 the Sears catalog stated, "Buying on Credit Is Folly." Like Sears, JCPenney department stores made millions annually on their plastic before they went bankrupt. But their founder, James Cash Penney, ran his retail empire with cash-only stores, large cash reserves, and zero debt—which helped the business survive the Great Depression. Henry Ford thought debt was a lazy man's method to purchase items, and his philosophy was so ingrained in Ford Motor Company that Ford didn't offer financing until 1959, ten years after General Motors did. Now, of course, Ford Motor Credit is one of the most profitable of Ford operations. The old school saw the folly of debt; the new school saw the opportunity to take advantage of the consumer with debt.

You have probably heard a lot of the sub-myths that fall in line behind the big one that says, "Debt is a tool." So that we leave no stone unturned, let's review and debunk each of the myths spread by a culture that has officially bought the lie.

MYTH: If I loan money to friends or relatives, I am helping them.

TRUTH: If I loan money to a friend or relative, the relationship will be strained or destroyed. The only relationship that would be enhanced is the kind resulting from one party being the master and the other party a servant.

The old joke is that if you loan your brother-in-law $100 and he never speaks to you again, was it worth the investment? We have all experienced loaning someone money and finding an immediate distancing in the relationship. Joan called my radio show one day complaining about how a loan had ruined her relationship with one of her best friends at work. She had loaned the lady, a broke single mom, $50 until payday. Payday came and went, and her friend—someone she used to talk to at lunch every day, someone who was her confidante and sounding board—now avoided her. Shame and guilt had entered the scene with no provocation. We don't control how debt affects relationships; debt does that independently of what we want. The borrower is slave to the lender, and you change the spiritual dynamic of relationships when you loan loved ones money. They are no longer a friend, uncle, or child; they are now your servant. I know some of you think that is overstated, but tell me why Thanksgiving dinner tastes different when a loan has been served. Eating with your master is different from eating with your family.

Joan was really torn up about losing this friendship. I asked her if the friendship was worth $50. She gushed that it was worth many times that, so I told her to call her friend and tell her the debt was forgiven, a gift. The forgiveness of the debt helped her remove the master-servant dynamic from the relationship. Of course, it would be better if that dynamic had never entered the scene. I also suggested two stipulations to the forgiveness of the debt: first, that the friend agrees to help someone in need someday; and second, that she never loan friends money. Let's break the myth chain. In Joan's case, the myth chain of loaning a friend money will be broken only if they both learn their lesson. The lesson is that while it is fine to *give* money to friends in need if you have it, loaning them money will mess up relationships.

I have dealt with hundreds of strained and destroyed families in which well-meaning people loaned money to "help." Parents loan the twenty-five-year-old newly married couple the down-payment money for the first home. It all seems so noble and nice until the daughter-in-law catches the disapproving glances at the mention of the couple's upcoming vacation. She knows the meaning of the glances, that she should check with these well-meaning, noble parents-in-law before she buys toilet paper until the loan is repaid. A lifetime of resentment can be born right there. The grandfather loans the twenty-year-old $25,000 to purchase that new four-wheel-drive truck he "needs." Of course, the loan is at 6 percent, much better than Junior can get at the bank and much better than Grandpa gets from his

CD at the bank. Everyone wins—or do they? What happens when Junior loses his job and can't pay Grandpa, who is from the old school where you dig ditches till midnight if you have to in order to honor your word? Now Junior and Grandpa are at odds, so Junior sells the truck and pays Grandpa the $19,000 he gets for it. Grandpa hadn't taken a lien on the title, so he now expects broke, angry, and unemployed Junior to repay the balance of $6,000. Grandpa will never see his $6,000 or his grandson again. In some perverted twist of the myth, mixed with shame and guilt, Junior's mind somehow concocts that this is all Grandpa's fault, and he abandons the relationship.

Hundreds of times I've seen relationships strained and sometimes destroyed. We all have, but we continue to believe the myth that a loan to a loved one is a blessing. It isn't; it is a curse. Don't put that burden on any relationship you care about.

MYTH: By cosigning a loan, I am helping a friend or relative.

TRUTH: Be ready to repay the loan; the bank wants a cosigner for a reason, which is that they don't expect the friend or relative to pay.

Think with me for a moment. If debt is the most aggressively marketed product in our culture today, if lenders must meet sales quotas for "loan production," if lenders can project the likelihood of a loan's going into default with unbelievable accuracy—all these things are true—and the lending industry has denied your friend or relative a loan, there is little doubt the potential borrower is trouble just looking for a place to happen. Yet people across America make the very unwise (yes, dumb) decision to cosign for someone else every day.

The lender requires a cosigner because there is a very high statistical chance that the applicant won't pay. So why do we appoint ourselves as the generous, all-knowing, benevolent helper to override the judgment of an industry that is foaming at the mouth to lend money, and yet has deemed our friend or relative a deadbeat looking for a place to fail, or at least a loan default looking for a new home? Why do we cosign knowing full well the inherent problems?

We enter this ridiculous situation only on emotion. Intellect could not take us on this ride. We "know" they will pay because we "know" them. Wrong. Parents cosign for a young couple to buy a home. Why do they need a cosigner? Because they couldn't afford the home! Parents cosign for a teenager to buy a car. Why would parents do this? "So he can learn to be responsible." No, what the teenager has learned is, if you can't pay for something, buy it anyway.

The sad thing is that those of us who have cosigned loans know how they end up. We end up paying them, but only after our credit is damaged or ruined. If you cosign for a car, the lender will not contact you when the loan is paid late every month, but your credit is damaged every month. The lender will not contact you before they repossess the car, but you now have a repo on your credit report. They will contact you to pay the difference between the debt and the below-wholesale repo price they got for the car, which is called a deficit. If the lender did contact you, there is nothing you can legally do to force the sale of the car, because you don't own it; you are merely on the hook for the debt. When you cosign on a house, you will get the same results.

According to Proverbs 17:18, "It's stupid to guarantee someone else's loan" (CEV). That pretty well sums it up. Just like trying to bless a loved one with a loan, many people are trying to help by cosigning, and the result is damaged credit and damaged or destroyed relationships. I have cosigned loans and ended up paying them; one poor guy cosigned for me, and he ended up paying when I went broke. If you truly want to help someone, give money. If you don't have it, then don't sign up to pay it, because you likely will.

I see cases of people caught in the cosigning trap every day on *The Ramsey Show*, our radio talk show. Kevin called to complain that a mortgage company was counting his cosigning for his mom's car against him as a debt even though she had insurance that would pay the loan if she died. Of course they count it, Kevin; it is a debt you are liable for! The mortgage company isn't worrying about her dying; they are worried about her not paying, which would require Kevin to make her car payments and then possibly not be able to pay his mortgage.

Joe, another caller, was surprised to find he was on the hook for $16,000 on a mobile home he cosigned for fifteen years ago. Ten years ago his brother's mobile home was repo'ed, and the bank sold it for $16,000 less than was owed; now, ten years later, the bank caught up with Joe and wanted its money. Joe was angry that this could happen! Most cosigners have no concept of the trip they've signed up for.

Brian emailed me about his girlfriend's car. It seems ol' Brian cosigned for a $5,000 car for his sweetie. Sweetie took off with the car, he can't find her, and, surprise of surprises, she isn't making the payments. Now either his credit shows him as a deadbeat or he makes payments on a car he can't find for a girl he doesn't want to find. That sums up cosigning: broken hearts and broken wallets. That's how cosigning usually goes, so unless you are looking for a broken heart and a broken wallet, do not do it.

MYTH: Cash advance, payday loans, rent-to-own, title pawning, and tote-the-note car lots.

TRUTH: These rip-off examples of predatory lending are designed to take advantage of lower-income people and benefit only the owners of the companies making the loans.

Lower-income people will remain at the bottom of the socioeconomic ladder if they fall for these rip-offs. These "lenders" (or, as I like to call them, "the scum of the scum") are bottom-feeders and legally make themselves rich on the backs of the poor or those soon to be poor. The average lending rates of these types of operations is nearly 400 percent interest and can be higher than 600 percent. If you want to stay on the bottom, keep dealing with these guys. You know why these types of operations are located only at the poor end of town? Because rich people won't play. That is how they got to be rich people.

The payday loan is one of the fastest-growing trash lenders out there. Here's how it works: You ask the lender for $200 and give them authorization to take money out of your account electronically after your next payday (or you can write them an old-fashioned paper check, postdated for your next payday). They will give you the $200 cash on the spot (or direct deposit the money into your account) and take out the money when you get paid. All for a mere $25 service charge, which equates to over 650 percent interest annually!

A guy named Mike called my radio show and was caught in a web of payday loans. He had not yet had a Total Money Makeover and was still spending like always. He kept adding loan after loan until he couldn't beat the shell game he had created. Basically, Mike was one of the 80 percent of borrowers who couldn't pay back his loan within two weeks. So he borrowed from one trash lender to pay another, and by doing this again and again, he had created a cycle of financial death. He was panicked because he was being threatened with criminal charges for writing bad checks by the very places that have a business model based on postdated "bad" checks. The sad thing is that the only way out for Mike is to pop the balloon. He has to stop paying them, close his accounts, and then meet with each lender to work out payment arrangements. That will mean extra jobs and selling things around the house.

This type of business is legalized loan sharking. Six states, Arizona, Arkansas, Georgia, Hawaii, New Mexico, and North Carolina, have legally run payday-loan businesses out of their state. Many others have capped the maximum size of the loans (most around $500), finance charges, and the amount of interest they can charge. Even the federal government recognized the problem and put a cap of 36 percent on payday loans made to military personnel. Hopefully other states will follow suit.

The classic tote-the-note car lot is no better. Most of these transactions involve older, cheaper cars. The dealer purchases these cars and sells them for a down payment equal to what he paid for the car, so the payments at 18 to 38 percent interest paid weekly are all gravy. Tow trucks all over town recognize these exact cars because the car being sold has been sold many times and repeatedly repo'ed by the dealer. Every time the dealer sells the car, his return on investment skyrockets. The payments could have purchased the car for cash in a matter of weeks; in fact, the down payment could have purchased the car if the buyer had been a little more savvy.

Rent-to-own is one of the worst examples of the little Red-Faced Kid in "I want it now!" mode. People rent items they can't possibly afford to buy because they look only at "how much a week" and think, *I can afford this.* According to *U.S. News & World Report*, you'll probably pay two to three times as much as you would just buying whatever it is outright! Well, when you look at the numbers, no one can afford this. The average, no-frills washer and dryer will cost you just $20 per week for 104 weeks. That is a total of more than $2,100 (not including tax) for a washer and dryer you could have bought new at full retail price for about $1,100 and slightly used for $500. As my old professor used to say about the "own" part of rent-to-own, "You should *live* so long!"

If you had saved $20 per week for just twenty-five weeks, you could have bought the scratch-and-dent model off the floor at the same rent-to-own store for $500! Or you could have bought a used set on Facebook Marketplace. It pays to look past the weekend and suffer through going to the local laundromat with your quarters. When you think short term, you always set yourself up for being ripped off by a predatory lender. If the Red-Faced Kid ("I want it, and I want it now!") rules your life, you will stay broke!

If you use payday loans, tote-the-note, and rent-to-own, please understand that you are being destroyed financially. These businesses feed on the working poor, and you must avoid them at all costs if you want to win with money.

MYTH: "Ninety days same as cash" equals using other people's money for free.

TRUTH: Ninety days is not the same as cash.

The silly marketing that America falls for has resulted in this: we buy things we don't need with money we don't have in order to impress people we don't like. "Ninety days same as cash" has exploded in furniture, electronics, and appliance sales. I recently met a lady who financed her dog at the pet store. "But I paid him off early," she said proudly. Good thing for Rover that he was able to avoid the repo man.

Ninety days is NOT the same as cash for three basic reasons: One, if you will flash cash ($100 bills) in front of a manager who has a sales quota to meet, you will likely get a discount. If you can't get a discount, go to the competitor and get one. You do not get the discount when you sign up for the finance plan.

Two, companies who offer same-as-cash financing make gobs of money off the people who don't pay them off in time. In 2021, these companies made $2.5 billion on the rip-off interest rates of 24 to 38 percent they back-charge to the date of purchase when the balance isn't paid in full by the end of the "promotional period." Please don't tell me you are the one who is actually going to pay it off and avoid becoming a victim of this billion-dollar scam. A $1,000 sound system (don't forget, you didn't get a discount) will not make you rich in ninety days. But $1,000 left in a savings account at 3 percent annual interest will earn you $7.50 in ninety days. Wow, some financial genius you are!

Three, you are playing with snakes, and you will get bitten. Marge called my radio show with this little story. She and her husband purchased a big-screen TV at a nationally known electronics store. This couple paid off the big screen slightly early to be sure they would not be tricked into the interest being back-charged. No such luck. They had declined the disability and life insurance (a charge of $174), but apparently the salesperson had fraudulently initialed the contract in that area, something that happens more frequently than you think. So although our brilliant couple thought they had paid off the TV, they still had a balance and were charged interest back through the entire deal. They were fighting it, but it would take hiring a handwriting expert and going to court with an attorney to avoid paying a bill under $1,000, even though they did not owe it. That is disheartening. The little game of "we are going to use your money for free" backfired big-time. I recently purchased a TV in that exact same store for cash; I got a discount and walked out with my TV. No hassle, no court costs, no interest, no lies.

No, Virginia, ninety days is NOT the same as cash.

And before you ask, no—buy now, pay later (BNPL) options like Klarna and Afterpay are no better. BNPL is a short-term loan that breaks up your purchase into four equal payments. It's just another way to buy stuff now you can't afford. But people are falling for it in droves. Total BNPL loan value is on track to reach $180 billion by 2025! Even worse, people aren't relying on BNPL to buy expensive laptops and gaming systems. They're using it more and more to pay for the essentials. That's right—you can use BNPL for your case of soda for just four easy payments of $2.99.

Some BNPL options only charge a late fee when you don't make your payments. Others charge interest. And our research shows nearly half of people don't make their payments on time. Oddly enough, that's about the same number of folks who regretted even making a BNPL purchase.

And the real dirty secret behind BNPL is that those companies use the fact that they can get you to spend more as a selling point with retailers. Afterpay brags that shoppers who use their services spend 40 percent more than people who don't. Klarna tells businesses that they can boost the average order price by 41 percent. And not to be shown up by its buddies in the business, Affirm boasts a 60 percent increase in upgrades, bundling, and add-ons! Is your stomach turning now?

MYTH: Car payments are a way of life; you'll always have one.

TRUTH: Staying away from car payments by driving reliable used cars is what the average millionaire does; that is how he or she became a millionaire.

Taking on a car payment is one of the dumbest things people do to destroy their chances of building wealth. The car payment is most folks' largest payment except for their home mortgage, so it steals more money from the income than virtually anything else. Experian notes that the average new car payment is $725 with an average term of about sixty-nine months. Most people get a car payment and keep it throughout their lives. As soon as a car is paid off, they get another payment because they "need" a new car. If you keep a $725 car payment throughout your life, which is "normal," you miss the opportunity to save that money. If you invested $725 per month from age twenty-five to age sixty-five, a normal working lifetime, in the average mutual fund averaging 12 percent (the ninety-year stock market average), you would have $8,500,000 at age sixty-five. Hope you like the car!

Some of you had your nose in the air as intellectual snobs when I illustrated how bad rent-to-own is because you would never enter such an establishment, and yet you are doing worse on your car deal. If you put $725 per month in a cookie jar for just ten months, you have more than $7,000 for a cash car. I am not suggesting you drive a $7,000 car your whole life, but that is how you start without debt. Then you can save the same amount again and trade up to a $14,000 car ten months later and up to a $21,000 car ten months after that. In just thirty months, or two and a half years, you can drive a paid-for $21,000 car, never having made a payment, and never have to make payments again. Taking on car payments because everyone else does it does not make it smart. Will your broke relatives and friends make fun of your junk car while you do this? Sure they will, but that is a very good sign you are on the right track.

Having been a millionaire and gone broke, I dug my way out by making a decision about looking good versus being good. Looking good is when your broke friends are impressed by what you drive, and being good is having more money than they have.

Are you starting to realize that The Total Money Makeover is also in your heart? You have to reach the point that what people think is not your primary motivator. Reaching the goal is the motivator. Do you remember the circus game where you swing the large hammer over your head to hit the lever to send a weight up a pole to ring the bell? You reach the point that you want to ring the bell! Who cares if you are a ninety-eight-pound weakling with gawky form? The girls are still impressed when the bell is rung. When the goal, not how you look, begins to matter, you are on your way to a Total Money Makeover.

Today I drive very nice cars, but it wasn't always that way. After going broke, I drove a borrowed 400,000-mile Cadillac with a vinyl roof torn loose so that it filled up with air like a parachute. The predominant color on this car was Bondo. I drove the Bondo buggy for what felt like ten years during one three-month period. I had dropped from a Jaguar to a borrowed Bondo buggy! This was not fun, but I knew that if I would live like no one else, later I could live like no one else. Today I am convinced that my wife and I are able to do anything we want financially partially because of the car sacrifices we made in the early days. I believe, with everything within me, that we are winning because of the heart change that allowed us to drive old, beat-up cars in order to win. If you insist on driving new cars with payments your whole life, you will literally blow a life's fortune on them. If you are willing to sacrifice for a while, you can have your life's fortune *and* drive quality cars. I'd opt for the millionaire's strategy.

MYTH: Leasing a car is what sophisticated people do. You should lease things that go down in value and take the tax advantage.

TRUTH: Consumer advocates, noted experts, and a good calculator will confirm that the car lease is the most expensive way to operate a vehicle.

Consumer Reports, *Smart Money* magazine, and my calculator tell me that leasing a car is the worst possible way to acquire a vehicle. In effect, you are renting to own. The cost of capital, which is the interest rate, is extremely high, yet most new car deals this year will be a fleece . . . I mean, a lease. They're *baaaadd*! Sorry. That's my impression of a sheep getting "fleeced." The auto industry lobbyists are so powerful that the law does not require full lender disclosure. The industry argues that you are merely renting, which you are, so they shouldn't be required to show you the actual effective interest rate. The Federal Trade Commission requires a truth-in-lending statement when you buy a car or get a mortgage, but not on a lease, so you don't know what you are paying unless you are very good with a calculator. Having seen several hundred lease agreements entered into by people I have counseled, my financial calculator confirms that the average interest rate is 14 percent.

Shouldn't you lease or rent things that go down in value? Not necessarily, and the math doesn't work on a car, for sure. Follow me through this example: If you rent (lease) a car with a value of $45,000 for three years, and when you turn it in at the end of that three-year lease the car is worth $22,500, someone has to cover the $22,500 loss. You're not stupid, so you know that General Motors, Ford, or any of the other auto giants aren't going to put together a plan to lose money. Your fleece/lease payment is designed to cover the loss in value ($22,500 spread over 36 months is equal to $625 per month), plus provide profit (the interest you pay).

Where did you get a deal in that? You didn't! On top of that, there is the charge of 15 to 30 cents per mile for going over the allotted miles and the penalties everyone turning in a lease has experienced for "excessive wear and tear," which takes into account every little nick, dent, carpet tear, smudge, or smell. You end up writing a large check just to walk away after renting your car. The whole idea of the back-end penalties is twofold: to get you to fleece/lease another one so you can painlessly roll the gotchas into the new lease, and to make sure the car company makes money.

According to J.D. Power, quoting the National Automobile Dealers Association (NADA), the average new car purchased for cash makes the dealer around 3.9 percent of the sticker price. So if you buy a new car for $50,000 (which is now the average price), the dealer will get almost $2,000. When the dealer can get you to finance with them, they tack on what's called a "finance reserve," or, in the case of a lease, they can mark up the "money factor," which effectively adds an extra 1–3 percentage points to your interest rate. That's another $1,600–$5,000 for the dealership. But the dealer doesn't have to tell you about the markup. And, worse, with a lease, the paperwork doesn't even show the sales price of the car. All you see is the "gross capitalized cost," which includes the dealer's profit margin and anything else they can sneak in without you noticing. And since you're getting such a great "deal" on the monthly payment, you don't notice or ask any questions. From there, they can get you to sign up for all kinds of add-ons like gap insurance and service plans where they'll make even more money off of you. The fact is, the typical car dealer makes their money in the finance office and the shop, not in the sale of new cars.

Car fleecing is exploding because dealers know it is their largest profit center. We live in a culture that quit asking, "How much?" and instead asks, "How much down, and how much a month?" If you look at only the monthly outlay, then you will always "fleece," because it almost always costs less down and less a month, but in the long run, it is much more expensive. Once again, the Red-Faced Kid bought something he couldn't afford using an unwise method and then attempted to justify his stupidity. That red-faced stuff won't work if you want a Total Money Makeover.

Craig called my radio show to argue about leasing because his CPA said he should lease a car. (Proof that some CPAs can't add, or at least don't take the time to!) Craig owned his own business and thought the tax write-off if his business owned the car made fleecing smart. Craig had the $20,000 cash to buy a one-year-old car just like the one he wanted, but instead he was going to fleece a new $30,000 one. He missed two important points. First, 98 percent of fleecing is done on a new car, which rapidly loses value—not a wise business decision. Second, creating an unneeded business expense for the sake of a tax write-off is bad math.

Let's say that Craig fleeced a car for $416 per month, $5,000 per year, and used it 100 percent for business (which is highly unlikely and most times won't survive an audit). If you have a tax write-off of $5,000, you don't pay taxes on that money. If Craig didn't have the $5,000 write-off, he would pay taxes on that $5,000, which would be about $1,100 in taxes. So Craig's CPA's suggestion that he send the car company $5,000 to keep from sending the government $1,100 sounds as though he can't add. Plus, Craig is now responsible for a $30,000 car that is dropping in value instead of a $20,000 car that took the worst drop in value during its first year.

My company owns my cars. We are able to straight-line depreciate those cars or write off the mileage. If you drive inexpensive cars in your business and put high mileage on them, take the mileage deduction. If you, like me, drive expensive cars but do not put many miles on them, take the straight-line depreciation. Both tax deductions are available to you without having a stupid car payment. If you don't own a business and didn't understand everything I just said about tax write-offs, etc., don't worry. Just know that, as a wise business owner, you don't want to fleece a car.

MYTH: You can get a good deal on a new car at 0 percent interest.

TRUTH: A new car loses 60 percent of its value in the first five years; that isn't 0 percent.

We have discussed the new-car purchase in its various forms for the last several pages. No, you can't afford a new car unless you are a millionaire and can, therefore, afford to lose thousands of dollars, all in the name of the neat new-car smell. A good used car that is less than three years old is as reliable or more reliable than a new car. A new $50,000 car will lose about $30,000 of value in the first five years you own it. That is about $115 per week in lost value. To understand what I'm talking about, open your window on your way to work once a week and throw out a $100 bill.

The average millionaire drives a two-year-old car with no payments. He or she simply bought it. The average millionaire is unwilling to take the loss that a new car dishes out; that is how they became millionaires. I am not saying you will never drive a brand-new car, but until you have so much money you can lose big bucks and not notice, you can't afford the luxury. The car dealer will tell you that you are "buying someone else's problems." Then why do they sell used cars? Wouldn't that be morally wrong? The truth is that most slightly used cars have gotten all the kinks worked out of them and were not traded because they were bad cars. In fact, there's a good chance you are buying a car that came off a lease. Some of the best car purchases I've made were one- and two-year lease turn-ins with low miles.

If you understand what I am saying about this huge loss in value, you now realize that 0 percent interest isn't really "no cost." While the money to borrow isn't technically costing you, you are losing so much in value that you have still been taken. Zero percent, however, is used quite often by guys (seldom gals) to rationalize their "need" for some new wheels. So even though the interest rate is attractive, pass it up because the whole transaction still means throwing $100 bills out the window each week.

Some people want to buy a new car for the warranty. If you lose $30,000 of value over five years, on average you have paid too much for a warranty. You could have completely rebuilt the car multiple times for $30,000! Also, keep in mind that most manufacturers' warranties will still cover you when buying a slightly used car. Of course, when you begin your Total Money Makeover, you may have an old beater, but the goal is to avoid the temptation of the 0 percent interest myth and get into quality used cars. (Still want to buy a new car? Sure they look great, smell great, and drive great—but the month-after-month and year-after-year payments definitely don't feel great.)

MYTH: You should get a credit card to build your credit.

TRUTH: You won't use credit with your Total Money Makeover, except maybe for a mortgage, and you don't need a credit card for that.

The best myth is the "build your credit" myth. Bankers, car dealers, and unknowledgeable mortgage lenders have told America for years to "build your credit." This myth means we have to get debt so we can get more debt because debt is how we get stuff. Those of us who have had a Total Money Makeover have found that cash buys stuff better than debt. But if I were selling debt, as the banker is, I also would tell you to get debt to get more debt. This is, however, a myth.

Yes, you will need to "build your credit" by borrowing and repaying debt in a timely fashion if you want to live a life of credit cards, student loans, and car payments. Not me. The one question we must answer is, "How do I get a home mortgage?" Later, I will introduce you to the 100-percent-down plan, or if you must, how to settle for a fifteen-year fixed-rate mortgage. But if you want that fifteen-year fixed rate with a payment that is no more than 25 percent of your take-home pay so I won't yell about it, don't you need credit? No.

You will need to find a mortgage company that does actual underwriting. Some mortgage companies call this a "no credit score" or "nontraditional credit" process. That means they are professional enough to process the details of your life instead of using only a FICO score (lending for dummies). It's getting harder to find a lender who will go to the trouble of actually getting to know you, but they're out there. If one bank tells you they can't do it, keep looking. You can get a mortgage if you have lived right. Let me define "lived right."

You can qualify for a conventional fifteen-year fixed-rate loan if:

- You have paid your landlord early or on time for two years.
- You have a history of uninterrupted, on-time payments for things like utility bills, insurance premiums, school tuition, childcare, or medical bills.
- You have been in the same career field for two years.
- You have a good down payment, which is more than "nothing down."
- You have no other credit, good or bad.
- You are not trying to take too big a loan. A payment that totals 25 percent of take-home pay is conservative and will help you qualify.

The FICO score is an "I love debt" score. According to the FICO website, your FICO score is determined by:

35 percent debt payment history
30 percent debt levels
15 percent length of debt
10 percent new debt
10 percent type of debt

So if you quit borrowing money you will lose your FICO score. It is not a score that says you are winning with money or that you have a million dollars; it mathematically says you LOVE DEBT. Please don't brag about your FICO score; that makes you look like you love playing kissy face with some bank. Dumb, dumb, dumb.

So can you get a mortgage without a FICO score? Many mortgage companies have gotten so lazy that FICO is the only lending they do. Others simply don't know how to write a loan without a score. But as of this writing, you can still get a mortgage with a zero score—it may just take a little longer to find a quality lender. You don't want to have a low score; it is best to have a high one or none at all. My personal score, by the way, is zero—because I haven't borrowed any money in decades.

MYTH: You need a credit card to rent a car, check into a hotel, or buy online.

TRUTH: A debit card will do all that.

The Visa debit card or other check cards that are connected to your checking account give you the ability to do virtually anything a credit card will do. I carry a debit card on my personal account and one on my business and do not have one credit card. Of course, you must have money before you can buy something with a debit card, but paying for things with money you have now is part of your Total Money Makeover. Most rental-car places don't take debit cards, but some do. Even though many will take the debit card, you need to check with the specific rental company in advance. Some of these places may make you jump through hoops to rent a car with debit, so do your research on their terms and conditions. All I'm saying is that it is possible. I buy things online and stay in hotels using my debit card all the time. In fact, I travel all over the nation several times a year speaking and doing appearances, and my debit card allows me access to the best things life has to offer with no debt.

Remember, there is one thing the debit card *won't* do: get you into debt.

MYTH: The debit card has more risk than a credit card.

TRUTH: Nope.

Some of you were concerned when I mentioned buying things online and reserving hotels with a debit card. The perception is that it's riskier to conduct that kind of business with a debit card. Supposed financial experts have spread this myth to the point that it is virtually urban legend. The fact is, Visa's regulations require the card-issuing bank to afford the debit card the exact same protections in cases of theft or fraud. If you have any doubt, read the liability information on Visa's own website. I contacted Visa directly and they sent this statement:

> Visa's Zero Liability policy covers all Visa credit—and debit-card transactions processed over the Visa network. Visa extends the same protections and benefits to its debit cards as it does to credit cards— including the ability for credit-card issuers to resolve merchant disputes on the cardholder's behalf if goods were defective or weren't received, you were overcharged, or for other reasons.

But remember, in order to get the full protection, be sure to run your card as a credit transaction—not using your PIN number. That's what I do.

MYTH: If you pay off your credit card every month, you get the free use of someone else's money.

TRUTH: Ramsey Solutions Research says that 61 percent of people don't pay off their credit cards every month.

As I said, when you play with snakes, you get bitten. I have heard all the bait put out there to lure the unsuspecting into the pit. A free hat, airline miles, brownie points back, free use of someone else's money, a discount at the register—the list goes on to get you to sign up for a credit card. Have you ever asked why they work so hard to get you involved? The answer is that you lose and they win.

You won't wear the hat, and according to CBSNews.com, as much as 92 percent of airline miles are never redeemed. The next time you are in the store that gave you a discount for signing up for a card, you will have forgotten your cash, you'll use the card, and the cycle begins. Maybe you think, *I pay mine off, so I'm using their money. I'm winning.* Wrong again. Decades of credit card research shows people spend 50–100 percent more when using credit instead of cash. Using credit actually activates the reward centers in your brain, so you spend more. But it hurts when you spend cash; therefore you spend less.

The big question is, what do millionaires do? They don't get rich with free hats, brownie points, air miles, and the use of someone else's money. What do broke people do? They use credit cards. According to an *American Journal of Public Health* Law and Ethics study of bankruptcy filers, 44 percent of filers say overspending, usually on credit cards, contributed to the bankruptcy. Broke people use credit cards; rich people don't. I rest my case.

Before getting on board with Dave's plan, I was so stressed with work and our financial situation that I ended up in the hospital with chest pains. My wife and I were making very good money in the San Francisco Bay Area, having nothing to show for it but lives under constant pressure. For years we had desired to move closer to our children and grandchildren, parents, and siblings. But the debt we carried would not allow us to move to a possibly lower-paying situation.

By the time we found *The Ramsey Show* on our daily long commutes to work, we were $95,000 in debt. It didn't take long for us to realize that he spoke truths laced with a strong dose of common sense. We destroyed the credit cards and set up a plan of attack following the Baby Steps as outlined in *The Total Money Makeover*. We paid off all consumer debt and cars within eighteen months, saved our six-month emergency fund, and had a plan to pay off the house within seven years.

A funny thing happened once we got rid of all that consumer debt: the stressful jobs were no longer a financial necessity. We didn't feel so much pressure on our lives either, and for the first time we could see a very bright light as we came out of the tunnel. Through Dave, God answered our prayers and allowed us to see clearly how we could move closer to our family!

We are now totally debt-free, including our home. We see family weekly and get to take part in all those wonderful events we had missed over the years. We are still saving 15 percent of our income and give with joy to church and charities in hopes that we can repay those blessings we have received and continue to receive.

We tell everyone who will listen to us about Dave and this great gift of financial peace. Getting rid of our credit cards and eliminating our outstanding debt on those cards freed us up to a point financially where we could take a pay cut and focus more on the things that really matter. My wife and I were happy before, but now we feel true joy in our lives.

Alan (age 48) and
Lonnie (age 47) Cluff
Both in Information Technology
Management

MYTH: Make sure your teenager gets a credit card so he or she will learn to be responsible with money.

TRUTH: Getting a credit card for your teenager is an excellent way to teach him or her to be financially irresponsible. That's why teens are now the number-one target of credit card companies.

The past several pages have been devoted to the evils of credit cards, so I'm not going to repeat myself in the case of teenagers. I'll only add that throwing your teen into a pool of sharks is a sure way to guarantee a lifetime of heartache for them and for you. I will also tell you that the vast majority of college seniors have credit card debt before they even have a job! The credit card marketers have done such a thorough job that a credit card is seen as a rite of passage into adulthood. American teens view themselves as adults if they have a credit card, a cell phone, and a driver's license. Sadly, none of these "accomplishments" are in any way associated with real adulthood.

You are not teaching your sixteen-year-old child to spend responsibly when you give him a credit card any more than you are teaching gun responsibility by letting him sleep with a loaded automatic weapon with the safety off. In both cases, you as a parent are being stupid. People with common sense don't give sixteen-year-olds beer to teach them how to hold their liquor. By giving a teenager a credit card, the parent, the one with supposed credibility, introduces a financially harmful substance and endorses its use, which is dumb but unfortunately very normal in today's families. Parents must instead teach the teenager to just say no. Anyone visiting a college campus in recent years has been shocked at the aggressive and senseless marketing of credit cards to people who don't have jobs. The results can be devastating. Two college students in Oklahoma gave up on their credit card debt and died by suicide with the bills lying on the bed beside them.

I got my first credit card when I was eighteen. Getting it felt like a rite of passage into adulthood, even though I didn't really know how it worked. I'm not sure I even understood that the money had to be paid back!

I ended up losing my job. The bills started piling up, so I moved out of my apartment and into my truck to save some cash. Then my truck got repossessed! For far too long, I used my credit cards to buy anything and everything. I wasn't budgeting at all, and I continued to treat credit card cash as income.

I got married and debt continued to cause my wife and me a lot of stress and worry. We were living in Section 8 housing—and my wife was scared to be there alone! We hoped that disaster wouldn't strike while we lived paycheck to paycheck. Without a buffer between us and life, we never knew when the next emergency would hit us.

I heard Dave on the radio, started his Baby Steps, and read *The Total Money Makeover*. We cut up our credit cards before we had an emergency fund in place, which made my wife nervous. We paid off $10,000 in debt on a $30,000 combined yearly income, and we are now debt-free!

We rarely disagree anymore when we create a budget. With each paycheck, we tithe, pay ourselves first (save!), pay bills, and use the envelope system for our other expenses. I ordered twenty copies of *The Total Money Makeover* and have enjoyed giving them away to my coworkers so they, too, can experience what it's like to be debt-free and have cash in hand for purchases. I've gone from being completely ignorant about my money to becoming debt-free and trying to help others gain financial peace!

**David (age 30) and
Tayelor (age 25) Jarrett**
*Technical Support Rep/Small Business
Owner; Clinical Assistant*

Vince called my radio show with a problem that has become a trend. Vince signed up for multiple cards during his sophomore year at college. He wasn't going to use the cards unless there was an emergency, but there was an "emergency" every week, and soon he was $15,000 in debt. He couldn't make the payments, so he quit school to get a job. The problem was, without his degree, his earnings were minimal. Worse than that, he also had $27,000 in student loans. Student loans aren't payable while you are in school, but when you leave school by graduating or quitting, the payments begin. Vince was one scared twenty-one-year-old with $42,000 in debt, but making only $31,000 per year. What's scary is that Vince is "normal."

The reason why lenders market so aggressively to teens is brand loyalty. The lenders' studies have found that we consumers are very loyal to the first bank that certifies our adulthood by issuing us plastic. When I am doing an appearance and cutting up credit cards, the emotional attachment many people have to the first card they got in college is amazing. They clutch it like it is an old friend. Brand loyalty is real.

Several thousand schools across America are using our high school curriculum called *Foundations in Personal Finance*. The results have been staggering. Teens latch on to *The Total Money Makeover* before they need one. A recent graduate of the program, fifteen-year-old Chelsea, said, "I think this class has totally changed my life. Whenever I see someone using a credit card, I think, *Whoa! How could they do that to their life?* I always thought you had to have credit card payments, house payments, and car payments. Now I realize you don't have to." Very cool, Chelsea.

Kid Branding

You have to start teaching kids early because "kid branding" is now commonplace. When my son was eleven years old, I looked at the back of a box of Raisin Bran and read "Visa . . . the official card of Whoville . . .

from *How the Grinch Stole Christmas*." I was not the target of this ad; my kid was. Lenders are teaching kids earlier and earlier their message of reliance on plastic. A few years back Mattel put out "Cool Shopping Barbie," which was sponsored by Mastercard. Of course, this "cool" babe had her own Mastercard. When she scanned her card, the cash register said, "Credit approved." There was so much consumer backlash that Mattel pulled the product. A few years ago Mattel came out with the "Barbie Cash Register," and apparently this lady does a lot of shopping. The register comes with its own American Express card. Why are these companies selling to our small children? Kid branding intends to influence card choices later in life. This is immoral.

Again, we decided to combat kid branding with our own antidote. *Financial Peace Jr.* is a collection of aids to help parents teach their children (ages three to twelve) about money. Of course, you can teach the principles without the kit, but either way, they need to learn them. In my home, we used the same techniques to teach our kids four things to do with money. We wanted to create teachable moments so that the kid branding would be counteracted by common sense. We taught our kids to work—not like being at some boot camp, but that doing chores equals money. Our kids were on commission, not allowance. Work and get paid; don't work and don't get paid. It's just like the real world. Our children put their newly earned money in envelopes labeled Save, Spend, and Give. When a child learns to work, save, spend, and give under a mature parent's direction, the child can avoid the messages that say a credit card equals prosperity.

MYTH: Debt consolidation saves interest, and you have one smaller payment.

TRUTH: Debt consolidation is dangerous because you treat only the symptom.

Debt CONsolidation—it's nothing more than a con because you think you've done something about the debt problem. The debt is still there, as are the habits that caused it; you just moved it! You can't borrow your way out of debt. You can't get out of a hole by digging out the bottom. Larry Burkett said debt is not the problem; it is the symptom. I feel debt is the symptom of overspending and undersaving.

A friend of mine works for a debt-consolidation firm whose internal statistics estimate that 78 percent of the time, after someone consolidates his credit card debt, the debt grows back. Why? Because he still doesn't have a game plan to either pay cash or not buy at all, and hasn't saved for "unexpected events," which will also become debt.

Debt consolidation seems appealing because there is a lower interest rate on some of the debt and a lower payment. In almost every case we review, though, we find that the lower payment exists not because the rate is actually lower but because the term is extended. If you stay in debt longer, you get a lower payment. If you stay in debt longer, you pay the lender more, which is why they are in the business of debt consolidation. The answer is not the interest rate; the answer is a Total Money Makeover.

MYTH: Borrowing more than my home's value is wise because I'll restructure my debt.

TRUTH: You are stuck in the house, which is really dumb.

On the radio show I took a call from a desperate man facing bankruptcy. He had borrowed $42,000 on a second mortgage, a home equity loan. Dan's existing balance on his first mortgage was $110,000, making his total new mortgage debt $152,000. Dan's home was worth $125,000, so he owed $27,000 more on his home than it was worth. He lost his job two months earlier and luckily had just found a job in another state, but he couldn't sell his home. He had the same job for sixteen years and thought he had security, but now, just a few months later, he was "in the soup."

My suggestion to Dan was that he call the second mortgage rip-off lender and get an acknowledgment of the truth, that there really isn't any collateral for the loan. They wouldn't foreclose in a hundred years, but they will sue him when the first mortgage company forecloses. So, after asking the second lender to release the lien for whatever proceeds above the first mortgage come from a sale, Dan will sign a note and make payments on the rest. Dan will have payments for years to come on a second mortgage for a home he no longer owns, but like most folks, his second mortgage was to pay off (move) debt he already had on credit cards, medical bills, and other life issues. Today, with a job in another state, Dan would rather have all his old debt back and his home where he could sell it easily.

MYTH: If no one used debt, our economy would collapse.

TRUTH: Nope, it would prosper.

The occasional economics teacher feels the need to pose this ridiculous scenario. My dream is to get as many Americans as possible out of debt with a Total Money Makeover. Unfortunately, I could sell ten million books, and there would still be seven billion credit card offers per year, so there is no danger of my working myself out of a job. The best weight-loss program in the world can never ensure there will be no fat Americans; after all, there are too many McDonald's.

However, let's pretend for the fun of it. What if every single American stopped using debt of any kind in one year? The economy would collapse. What if every single American stopped using debt of any kind over the next fifty years, a gradual TOTAL Money Makeover? The economy would prosper, although banks and other lenders would suffer. Do I see tears anywhere? What would people do if they didn't have any payments? They would save and they would spend, not support banks. Spending by debt-free people would support and prosper the economy. The economy would be much more stable without the tidal waves caused by "consumer confidence" or the lack thereof. (Consumer confidence is that thing economists use to measure how much you will overspend due to your being giddy about how great the economy is, never taking into consideration that you are going deeply into debt. If the consumer were out of debt and living within his means, the confidence he would have would be well-founded.) Saving and investing would cause wealth to be built at an unprecedented level, which would create more stability and spending. Giving would increase, and many social problems would be privatized; thus, the government could get out of the welfare business. Then taxes could come down, and we would have even more wealth. Ahhhh, isn't capitalism cool? Those who are worried about polarization, the widening gap between the haves and the have-nots, need not look to government to solve the problem; just call for a national Total Money Makeover.

Debt Is *Not* a Tool

Are you beginning to understand that debt is NOT a tool? This myth and all its little sub-myths have been spread far and wide. Always keep in mind the idea that if you tell a lie often enough, loud enough, and long enough, the myth becomes accepted as a fact. Repetition, volume, and longevity will twist and turn a myth, a lie, into a commonly accepted way of doing things. No more. Debt is not a tool; it is a method to make banks wealthy, not you. The borrower truly is slave to the lender.

Your largest wealth-building asset is your income. When you tie up your income, you lose. When you invest your income, you become wealthy and can do anything you want.

How much could you give every month, save every month, and spend every month if you had no payments? Your income is your greatest wealth-building tool, not debt. Your Total Money Makeover begins with a permanently changed view of the debt myths.

4

Money Myths: The (Non) Secrets of the Rich

Most money myths have to do with a lie about a shortcut or a lie about safety. We yearn to become healthy, wealthy, and wise with no effort and with no risk, but it will never happen. Why else is the lottery so successful in pulling in millions of dollars? Why do people stay in jobs they hate, seeking false security? The Total Money Makeover mentality is to live like no one else so later we can live like no one else. A price has to be paid, and there are no shortcuts. While no one goes looking for needless pain, risk, or sacrifice, when something sounds too good to be true, it is. The myths in this chapter are rooted in two basic problems. First is risk denial, thinking total safety is possible and likely. Second is easy wealth, or looking for the magic key to open the treasure chest.

Risk Denial

Risk denial takes several forms in the world of money. Sometimes risk denial is a kind of laziness, when we don't want to take the energy to realize that energy is needed to win. Other times risk denial is a kind of surrender in which we settle for a bad solution because we are so beat down or beat up that we wave the white flag and do something stupid. At still other times, risk denial can have an active component when we search for a false security that simply doesn't exist. This is the risk denial of someone who keeps a job he or she hates for fourteen years because the company is "secure," only to find life turned upside down by a layoff when the "secure" company files for bankruptcy. Money denial always involves an illusion, followed by disillusionment.

Quick, Easy Money

The second underlying problem is the quest for easy wealth. Quick, easy money is one of the oldest lies, or myths, in the book of the human race. A shortcut, a microwave dinner, instant coffee, and lottery millionaires are things we wish would give us high quality, but they never do. The secrets of the rich don't exist, because the principles aren't a secret. There is no magic key, and if you are looking for one, you've set yourself up for pain and the loss of money. One of my pastors says that living right is not complicated; it may be difficult, but it is not complicated. Living right financially is the same way—it is not complicated; it may be difficult, but it is not complicated.

Myth vs. Truth

In addition to debt myths, we must dispel several other money myths as part of your Total Money Makeover. Most of these money myths are rooted in the problems we have already discussed: denial and/or a shortcut mentality.

MYTH: Everything will be fine when I retire. I know I'm not saving yet, but it will be okay.

TRUTH: The cavalry isn't coming.

How can I put this delicately? There is no shining knight headed your way on a white horse to save the day. Wake up! This is the real world where sad old people eat Alpo! Please don't be under the illusion that this government, one that is so inept and dim-witted with money, is going to take great care of you in your golden years. That is your job! This is an emergency! The house is on fire! You have to save. You have to invest in your future. You won't be FINE! Do you get the picture?

We live in the land of plenty, and that has until recently lulled a large percentage of Americans to sleep, thinking everything will be "okay." Things won't be okay unless you make them that way. Your destiny and your dignity are up to you. You are in charge of your retirement. We'll talk about how to take charge of it later in the book, but for now, you'd better be 100 percent convinced that this area deserves your full attention *right now*—not tomorrow or pretty soon. Personally, I don't want to work at McDonald's when I retire—unless it's the one I own on St. Thomas in the U.S. Virgin Islands.

MYTH: Gold is a good investment and will cover me if the economy collapses.

TRUTH: Gold has a poor track record and isn't used when an economy collapses.

Gold has been sold as a stable investment that everyone should own. Conventional wisdom intones, "Since the beginning of time, gold has been the standard that man has used to exchange goods and services." After making that pitch, the mythsayer will follow up with the statement that in a failed economy, gold is the only thing that will retain its value. "You will have what everyone wants" is how the pitch continues. After hearing these pitches, people buy gold as an investment under the illusion of false security, or risk denial.

The truth is that gold is a lousy investment with a long track record of mediocrity. The average rates of return tracked as far back as Napoleon are around 2 percent gain per year. In recent history, gold has a fifty-year track record of around 7.8 percent. During that same time frame, you would have made around 12 percent in a good growth-stock mutual fund. During those fifty years, though, there has been incredible volatility and tons of risk.

While gold has done very well since 2001, this is the only period in history that it has seen great rates of return. And most of those returns are based on the doomsayer emotions brought on by 9/11 and the Great Recession and the COVID pandemic.

It is also important to remember that gold is not used when economies fail. History shows that when an economy completely collapses, the first thing that appears is a black-market barter system in which people trade items for other items or services. In a primitive culture, items of utility often become the medium of exchange, and the same is temporarily true in a failed economy. A skill, a pair of blue jeans, or a tank of gas becomes very valuable, but not gold coins or nuggets. Usually a new government rises from the ashes, and new paper money or coinage is established. Gold will, at best, play a minor role, and the gold investor will be left with the sick feeling that real estate, canned soup, or knowledge would have been a better hedge against a failed economy.

MYTH: I can get rich quickly and easily if I join these groups, go to this seminar, subscribe to this service, and work three hours a week.

TRUTH: No one develops and makes a six-figure income on three hours a week.

I received an email recently from a gentleman offering me a five hundred-to-one return on my money. He stated that he has become so enthused about the prospects of this "investment" that he has gotten several of his friends in the deal with him. (Oh no.) He didn't have a lot of time in his busy schedule, but he would make time if I would meet with him. No thanks. I don't know what this is, but I know it is a scam. I am not cynical, but I do know investments. Odds of five hundred to one don't come through, and I won't waste my time discussing them or trying to find the flaw in the logic. It is a scam, period. Run as fast as you can to get away from these people!

As a younger man I often fell prey to this type of garbage. Later, I used to have meetings with these guys to try to find the flaw. Now I just shake my head—because I know he is heading for pain and loss, and so are his friends.

Have you seen the midnight infomercials about a seminar in some exotic location where a guy fills you in on the "secrets" so that "you too" can become wildly wealthy by buying nothing-down real estate or by learning the hidden formula to success in the stock market? Small-business ideas abound, such as getting rich at home by stuffing envelopes and doing medical billings. Be realistic. Envelopes are stuffed by machines at a rate of thousands a minute and at a cost of tenths of a penny; they are not stuffed by a stay-at-home mom trying to supplement the family income! One person in every thousand who attempts the oversold, overdone medical-billing concept does so at a profit. The legitimate, profitable medical biller is usually someone who came from the medical industry, not someone who got ripped off taking a weekend course. Don't fall for this!

Real estate can be purchased for nothing down, but then you owe so much on it that there is no cash flow. You have to "feed" it every month. I bought foreclosure and bankruptcy real estate for years and know it can be done, but the players with cash are the ones who win. The good deals are one in two hundred *if* you are experienced and very good at the business; I worked sixty hours a week, and it took me years to get to a six-figure income in real estate.

The stock market attracts the brightest business minds on the planet. These mega-nerds study, track, chart, eat, and breathe the stock market, and have for generations. Still, every other year a book or con artist comes out claiming to have "discovered" little-known keys, patterns, or trends that will "make you rich." The Beardstown Ladies published a *New York Times* bestseller about their cute little quilting group who started investing and discovered how to get unbelievable returns. As it turns out, the whole thing was a fraud; they never got those reported returns, and the publisher got sued. Another book was published on the Dogs of the Dow, showing a little-known pattern about buying the worst stocks on the Dow Jones Industrial Average to gain wealth. As it turns out, the author wrote another book about how to invest in bonds after he had discovered his formula didn't work.

It is really hard to sell books and digital courses that teach the necessity of lots of hard work, living on less than you make, getting out of debt, and living on a plan, but I'm trying—because it's the only way that will work. Meanwhile, the sooner you understand that no one gets rich quick by using secret information, the better.

MYTH: Cash value life insurance, like whole life, will help me retire wealthy.

TRUTH: Cash value life insurance is one of the worst financial products available.

Sadly, more than 60 percent of the life insurance policies sold today are cash value policies. A cash value policy is an insurance product that packages insurance and savings together. Do not invest money in life insurance; the returns are horrible. Your insurance person will show you wonderful projections, but none of these policies perform as projected.

Let's look at an example. If a thirty-year-old man has $100 per month to spend on life insurance and shops the top five cash value companies, he will find he can purchase an average of $125,000 in insurance for his family. The pitch is to get a policy that will build up savings for retirement, which is what a cash value policy does. However, if this same guy purchases twenty-year level term insurance with coverage of $125,000, the cost will be only $10 per month, not $100. Wow. If he goes with the cash value option, the other $90 per month should be in savings, right? Well, not really; you see, there are expenses. Expenses? How much? All of the $90 per month disappears in commissions and expenses for the first two to five years; after that, the return will average around 2 percent per year for whole life, between 3 and 4.5 percent for universal life, and maybe slightly better returns on a variable life policy that includes mutual funds. No matter how you slice it, this product is a really bad idea!

Worse yet, with whole life and universal life, the savings you finally build up after being ripped off for years don't go to your family upon your death; the only benefit paid to your family is the face value of the policy, $125,000 in our example. The truth is that you would be better off getting a $10 term policy and putting the extra $90 in a cookie jar! At least after three years you would have $3,000, and when you died your family would get your savings.

As you continue in this book and learn how to have a Total Money Makeover, you will begin investing well. Then, when you are fifty-seven and the kids are grown and gone, the house is paid for, and you have $700,000 in mutual funds, you'll become self-insured. That means when your twenty-year term is up, you shouldn't need life insurance at all—because with no kids to feed, no house payment, and $700,000, your spouse will just have to suffer through if you die without insurance.

MYTH: Playing the lottery and other forms of gambling will make you rich.

TRUTH: The lottery is a tax on the poor and on people who can't do math.

One day I was in a lottery state for a speaking engagement. I went into the gas station to pay for my fill-up and saw a line of people. For a moment I thought I was going to have to stand in line to pay for my gas, before I realized that the line was for purchasing lottery tickets. Have you ever seen those lines? Next time you do, look at the people in the line. Darryl and his other brother Darryl. These are not rich people, and these are not smart people. The lottery is a tax on poor people and on people who can't do math. Rich people and smart people would be in the line if the lottery were a real wealth-building tool, but the truth is that the lottery is a rip-off instituted by our government. This is not a moral position; it is a mathematical, statistical fact. Studies show that the zip codes that spend four times what anyone else does on lottery tickets are those in lower-income parts of town. The lottery, or gambling of any kind, offers false hope, not a ticket out. A Total Money Makeover offers hope because it works. Remember, I have been broke twice in my life, but never poor; poor is a state of mind.

Gambling represents false hope and denial. Energy, thrift, and diligence are how wealth is built, not dumb luck.

MYTH: Mobile homes, or trailers, will allow me to own something instead of renting, and that will help me become wealthy.

TRUTH: Trailers go down in value rapidly, making your chances for wealth building less than if you had rented.

Trailers go down in value rapidly. People who buy a $150,000 double-wide home will in five years owe $132,000 on a trailer worth $100,000. Financially, it's like living in your new car. If I were to suggest you invest $150,000 into a mutual fund with a proven track record of dropping to $100,000 in just five years, you would look at me as if I had lost my mind. I am not above living in a mobile home. I have lived in worse. I just know mobile homes are lousy places to put money. You'll see reports these days that say mobile homes actually appreciate in value at a similar pace as regular single-family homes. Don't be fooled. Those reports are based on mobile homes titled as real property, which means they are permanently attached to the land. The value of the land is going up, not the value of the trailer. If it walks like a duck and quacks like a duck, it is a duck. Call it "manufactured housing," put it on a permanent foundation, add lots of improvements around the yard, and it is still a trailer when you are ready to sell it.

I want you to own a home because homes are a good investment. The fastest way to become a homeowner is through a Total Money Makeover while renting the cheapest thing you can suffer through. The purchase of a trailer is not a shortcut but a setback on the path to owning real estate that goes up in value. If the typical consumer considering buying your home can walk up and tell it was ever a trailer in any form, your home will go down, not up, in value.

The only exception to the "no trailers" rule is Ron's plan. Ron graduated from *Financial Peace University* and was on track for a Total Money Makeover. Ron and his wife prayerfully decided to sell their nice $120,000 home on which they owed only $50,000. They bought a small farm and a very used $3,000 trailer. With no payments and an income of $85,000, they saved and built a very nice, paid-for $250,000 home in just a couple of years. The appraisal was $250,000, but since they paid cash for the land, they got a bargain. Also, as a contractor Ron built the home for pennies on the dollar, so it didn't take them long to finish paying for the home. They sold the $3,000 trailer for $3,200; after all, $3,000 trailers have lost about all their value, so the sale comes down to negotiating.

MYTH: Prepaying my funeral or my kids' college expenses is a good way to invest and protect myself against inflation.

TRUTH: Plans for prepaid funerals and college expenses give low rates of return and put money in the other guy's pocket.

When you prepay something, your return on investment (interest) is the amount the item will go up in value before you use it. In other words, by prepaying, you avoid the price increases, and that is your return. Prepaying items is like investing at the item's inflation rate. For example, prepaying college tuition will save you the amount tuition goes up between the time you lock in and the time your child begins his college education. The average inflation rate for tuition nationally is about 8 percent, so prepaying tuition is like investing money at 8 percent. That is not bad, but mutual funds will average about 12 percent over a long period of time, and you can save for college tax-FREE. (More about college saving later in your Total Money Makeover.)

The same concept is true for prepaid burial plans. If you have gone through the gut-wrenching exercise of selecting a casket, burial plot, and so on in the middle of grief, you don't want loved ones to experience the same. Preplanning the details of your funeral is wise, but prepaying is unwise. Sara's mom died suddenly, and the grief was overwhelming. In the midst of that pain, Sara felt they made unwise purchases as part of the funeral arrangements, and she vowed not to leave her family in the same predicament. So Sara, age thirty-nine, paid $8,000 for a prepaid funeral. Again, it is wise to preplan, not to prepay. Why? If she were to invest $8,000 in a mutual fund averaging 12 percent, upon an average death age of seventy-eight, Sara's mutual fund would be worth $842,300! I think Sara could be buried for that, with a little left over, unless, of course, she is King Tut!

MYTH: I don't have time to work on a budget, retirement plan, or estate plan.

TRUTH: You don't have time not to.

Most people concentrate on the urgent in our culture. We worry about our health and focus on our money only after they're gone. Dr. Stephen

Covey's book *The Seven Habits of Highly Effective People* examines this problem. Dr. Covey says one of the habits of highly effective people is that they begin with the end in mind. Wandering through life aimlessly will bring you much frustration.

Covey says to divide activities into four quadrants. Two of the quadrants are Important/Urgent and Important/Not Urgent. The other two are Not Important, so let's skip those. We take care of the Important/Urgent stuff, but what is Important/Not Urgent in a Total Money Makeover is planning. You can pay the electric bill or sit in the dark, but if you don't do a monthly spending plan, there is no apparent immediate damage.

John Maxwell has the best quote on budgeting I have ever heard. I wish I had said it: "A budget is people telling their money where to go instead of wondering where it went." You have to make your money behave, and a written plan is the whip and chair for the money tamer.

Earl Nightingale, motivational legend, said that most people spend more time picking out a suit of clothes than planning their careers or even their retirements. What if your life depended on how you managed your 401(k) or whether you started your Roth IRA today? Actually, it does—because the quality of your life at retirement depends on your becoming an expert in money management today.

Estate planning is never urgent until someone dies. You must think long term to win with money, and that includes thinking all the way through death. More on this later, but just remember, everyone must budget, plan retirement, and do estate planning—everyone.

MYTH: Debt-management companies on TV, like American Consumer Credit Counseling, will save me.

TRUTH: You may get out of debt, but only with your credit trashed.

Debt-management companies are springing up everywhere. These companies "manage" your debt by taking one monthly payment from you and distributing the money among your creditors, with whom they've often worked out lower payments and lower interest. This is not a loan, as with debt consolidation. Sometimes people get the two confused. Both are bad, but we have already covered the debt consolidation loans. However, because America needs a Total Money Makeover, the debt-management business has become one of the fastest-growing industries today. Companies like American Consumer Credit Counseling can help you get better interest rates and lower payments, but at a price. When you use one of these companies and then try to get a conventional, FHA, or VA loan, don't be surprised when your lender declines your application or requires it to go through manual underwriting before coming back with a sky-high interest rate. A debt-management plan is a big red flag to lenders that screams you're a high-risk borrower. They will consider your credit trashed, so don't do it.

Another problem with debt management by someone else is that your habits don't change. You can't have someone lose weight for you; you have to change your exercise and diet habits. Handling money is the same way; you have to change your behavior. Turning all your problems over to someone else treats the symptom, not the problem.

Our firm does financial counseling and trains counselors around the nation for referrals. We will not handle your money for you. We lead you into a mandatory Total Money Makeover. We are not babysitters. We have had thousands of clients over the years who have gone to debt-management companies for help. When the clerk taking the order couldn't make the person's life fit their cookie-cutter computer program, the customer was advised to file for bankruptcy. After we met with them, it was obvious that the customer wasn't bankrupt; they just needed radical "surgery." Don't take bankruptcy advice from debt-management companies; you likely aren't bankrupt.

The worst abuser in this industry has now been put out of business.

AmeriDebt was started by Andris Pukke, who, prior to beginning this business, pled guilty to federal charges of defrauding customers in a debt-consolidation loan scam. In spite of this, AmeriDebt grew to revenues of $40 million and spent $15 million per year getting you to use their services. They were so blatant in their misleading of consumers that the Federal Trade Commission (FTC) finally stepped in and shut them down. The FTC says hidden fees and deceptive practices took over $170 million out of Americans' pockets. In the largest case of this type ever, the FTC took a $170 million judgment against AmeriDebt, which is now in bankruptcy. Andris Pukke is court-ordered to give up $35 million in personal assets to settle with consumers. There are truly sharks out there.

MYTH: I can buy a kit to clean up my credit, and all my past misdeeds will be washed away.

TRUTH: Only inaccuracies can be cleaned from credit reports, so this is a scam.

The Federal Fair Credit Reporting Act dictates how consumers and creditors interact with the credit bureaus. Bad credit drops off your credit report after seven years unless you have a Chapter 7 Bankruptcy, which stays on for ten years. Your credit report is your financial reputation, and you can't have anything taken off your report unless the item is inaccurate. If you have an inaccuracy that needs to be removed, you need to write a letter pointing out the error and ask them to correct this error right away. Accurate bad credit stays unless you lie. Lying for the purpose of getting money is fraud. Don't do it.

Credit-repair companies are largely scams. The Federal Trade Commission regularly conducts raids to close down these fraudulent companies. I have had many callers on my radio show who purchased a $300 kit to "clean" their credit. Sometimes the kit tells you to dispute all bad credit and ask to have it removed even if the item is reported accurately. Don't do that. The worst idea the kits push is to get a new Social Security number. By getting a second identity, you get a brand-new credit report, and lenders

> **DAVE RANTS...**
>
> I am not against the enjoyment of money. What I am against is spending money when you do not have money to begin with.

will never know about your past misdeeds. This is fraud, and if you do this, you will go to jail. Do not pass go; go directly to jail—fraud. You are lying to get a loan, which is not credit cleanup, and this is criminal.

Clean your credit with a Total Money Makeover. I will show you how to live under control and pay cash for stuff so you don't need credit, and over time your credit will clean itself.

MYTH: My divorce decree says my spouse has to pay the debt, so I don't.

TRUTH: Divorce decrees do not have the power to take your name off credit cards and mortgages, so if your spouse doesn't pay, be ready to. You still owe the debt.

Divorce happens a lot, and it is truly sad. Divorce means we split up everything, including the debts; however, the debts are not easily split. If your name is on a debt, you are liable to pay it, and your credit is affected if you don't. A divorce court does not have the power to take your name off a debt. The divorce judge only has the power to tell your spouse to pay it for you. If your spouse doesn't pay, you can tell the judge, but you are still liable. A lender who doesn't get paid will correctly report bad credit on all parties to the loan, including you. A lender who doesn't get paid can correctly sue the parties to the loan, including you.

If your ex-husband keeps his truck that you both signed for and then doesn't make the payments, your credit is damaged, the truck gets repo'ed, and you will get sued for the balance. If you quitclaim-deed your ownership in the family home to your ex-wife as part of the settlement, you will find yourself in a mess. A quitclaim deed is the easy way to give up ownership in your home. If she doesn't pay on time, your credit is trashed; if she gets foreclosed on, so have you. Even if she pays perfectly on the home or he does on the truck, you will find that you have trouble buying the next home because you have too much debt.

If you are going to leave a marriage, make sure that all debts are refinanced out of your name or force the sale of the item. Don't have the attitude: "I don't want to make him sell his truck." If you are that much in love, don't get divorced; but if you are walking away, make it a complete, clean break even though it's painful now. I have counseled thousands of people who were broken financially by ex-spouses and bad advice from a divorce attorney. So sell the house or refinance it as part of the divorce, period. The only other option is mega-risk, and you can count on heartache and even more anger coming your way.

MYTH: That collector was so helpful; he really likes me.

TRUTH: Collectors are not your friends.

There are a few good collectors, very few. Almost every time a collector is "understanding," or wants to "be your friend," there is a reason: to get you to pay your bill. The other technique is to be mean and nasty, and you may find your new "friend" using all kinds of bullying tactics once you have a "relationship."

Your Total Money Makeover will cause you to pay your debts. I want you to pay what you owe, but collectors are not your friends. Credit-card collectors are the worst, for they will lie, cheat, and steal—and that is just before breakfast. You can tell if a credit-card collector is lying by looking to see if his lips are moving. Any deal, special plan, or settlement you make with collectors must be in writing BEFORE you send them money. Otherwise, you will find that you don't have a deal, that they lied. Never allow collectors electronic access to your checking account, and never send postdated checks. They will abuse you if you give them this power, and there will be nothing you can do, because you owe them money. Clear?

MYTH: I'll just file bankruptcy and start over; it seems so easy.

TRUTH: Bankruptcy is a gut-wrenching, life-changing event that causes lifelong damage.

Kathy called my radio show, ready to file bankruptcy. Her debts were overwhelming, and her cheating husband had left with his girlfriend. The house was in his name, as was all the debt except $11,000. Kathy was twenty years old, and her brilliant uncle, a lawyer from California, told her to file bankruptcy. Kathy was beat up, beat down, and deserted, but she was not bankrupt. When her soon-to-be ex-husband ends up with all the debt in his name, he may be bankrupt, but Kathy wasn't.

Bankruptcy is not something I recommend any more than I would recommend divorce. Are there times when good people see no way out and file bankruptcy? Yes, but I will still talk you out of it if given the opportunity. Few people who have been through bankruptcy would report that it is a painless wiping-clean of the slate, after which you merrily trot off into your future to start fresh. Don't let anyone fool you. I have been bankrupt and have worked with the bankrupt for decades, and it is not a place you want to visit.

Bankruptcy is listed in the top five life-altering negative events that we can go through, along with divorce, severe illness, disability, and the loss of a loved one. I would never say that bankruptcy is as bad as losing a loved one, but it is life-altering and leaves deep wounds both to the psyche and the credit report.

Chapter 7 Bankruptcy, which is total bankruptcy, stays on your credit report for ten years. Chapter 13 Bankruptcy, more like a payment plan, stays on your credit report for seven years. Bankruptcy, however, is for life. Loan applications and many job applications ask if you have ever filed for bankruptcy. Ever. If you lie to get a loan because your bankruptcy is very old, technically you have committed criminal fraud.

Most bankruptcies can be avoided with a Total Money Makeover. Your Total Money Makeover may involve extensive amputation of stuff, which will be painful, but bankruptcy is much more painful. If you take the thoughtful step backward to get on solid ground instead of looking at the false allure of the quick fix that bankruptcy seems to offer, you will win more quickly and easily. I know from personal experience the pain of bankruptcy, foreclosure, and lawsuits. Been there, done that, got the T-shirt, and it is not worth it.

We've never handled money well at all. I guess that's a bit of an understatement—we've filed bankruptcy three times!

The first time we filed, we felt like bankruptcy was our only option. Our small-business loan to buy a body shop went from 4 percent to 22 percent APR, and we lost all our earnest money. Soon after, my husband had his first heart attack, and other problems seemed to pile on. Before long, we lost our house and cars. We moved to a different state with four kids, two cats, a dog, a motorcycle, a U-Haul trailer, $800—and no jobs.

We were depressed and felt like failures as we put our life back together. You'd have thought we would have learned our lesson, right? Wrong.

Instead of learning from our mistakes, we actually repeated the whole thing again a little over a decade later. After an injury due to a fall, my husband was out of work for six months. Our income went from $4,000 a week to $400 a week. We racked up credit-card debt and ended up filing bankruptcy a second time. Again, we lost our house and most of our possessions.

Although the first bankruptcy felt like the end of the world, the second one didn't upset us too much. We felt like it wasn't a big deal because we'd been down that road before. So we just started over a third time, still making the same bad choices.

Over the next seven years, we started a new business, made a lot of poor decisions, and closed yet another company. Then we filed bankruptcy a third time. After filing, we were ashamed and too embarrassed to tell anyone. We had this awful, dirty secret that we hid from our family and friends. To make matters worse, all the stress and shame caused my husband to have two more heart attacks.

Going through the bankruptcy process was horrible. No one will meet your eye in the trial room. It's like everyone has the plague and is afraid to talk to anyone. Filing bankruptcy three times made us feel like a fraud. We wondered, *What's wrong with us? Why do we keep repeating the same mistakes?*

When our son came home from deployment with a mental illness, we became his full-time caretakers. Money was extremely tight because we were caring for our son on only one income—my husband had retired after his third heart attack. We were close to filing bankruptcy for a fourth time when my daughter came to our rescue by introducing us to Dave Ramsey.

Now, we're on The Total Money Makeover plan and trying to make a dent in our financial mess. It's tough trying to correct a lifetime of bad decisions and behaviors about money! But even though we've restarted Baby Step One three times, we've still been able to pay off $26,000 of debt! Finally, we have hope for our future, and we are motivated to help others so they don't go down the same path we did.

Susan (age 52) and
Larry (age 67) Hickman
Collection Manager, Retired Insurance Broker

We teach people to carry cash. In a culture where the salesclerk thinks you are a drug dealer if you pay with cash, I know this suggestion may seem weird. However, cash is powerful. If you carry cash, you spend less, and you can get bargains by flashing cash. Linda emailed my newspaper column, complaining that she would get robbed if she carried cash. I explained to her that crooks don't have x-ray vision to look into her pocket or purse. The crooks assume that your purse is like all the others filled with credit cards that are over the limit. Look, I'm not making light of crime. There's a chance you may get robbed, because people do get robbed—whether they carry cash or not. And if it happens to you, the cash will be taken. But, trust me, you need to be far more worried about the danger of using credit cards than the danger of being robbed while carrying cash. Carrying cash doesn't make you more likely to get robbed; on the contrary, the mismanagement of plastic is robbing you every month.

MYTH: I can't use cash because it is dangerous; I might get robbed.

TRUTH: You are being robbed every day by not using the power of cash.

We have already destroyed the myth of credit cards and shown that when you spend cash, you spend less. When you put together your written game plan, you will find that managing spending categories as part of your Total Money Makeover is a must to gain control. Cash enables you to say no to yourself. When the food envelope is getting low on cash, we eat leftovers instead of ordering pizza again.

MYTH: I can't afford insurance.

TRUTH: Some insurance you can't afford to be without.

DAVE RANTS...

Breaking Down the Envelope System

It's easy to overspend when you don't have a clear boundary line. The budget tells you what that line is for each category, but when your gas money and grocery money and entertainment money are all sitting in one big lump in your bank account, one category can plow right past the line without you knowing. That's why I recommend using the envelope system for some categories.

Say you budget $600 for food this month. Well, when you get paid, you take that $600 out of the bank in cash—yes, actual *cash*—and put it in an envelope. Write "FOOD" on the outside of that envelope. When you go to the store, take your envelope and spend your cash.

You don't use that money for anything other than food, and you don't buy any food except with the money out of that envelope. When the cash is gone, you're done! That's a pretty clear boundary!

The envelope system works best in categories like food, entertainment, clothing, gas—stuff like that. You don't need to use it for monthly bills that you send through the mail or have automatically debited from your account.

Here's the deal: Swiping a piece of plastic doesn't register in your brain the same way cash does. When you actually lay a couple of Benjamins on the counter, you *know* you're spending money! That's why using the envelope system will help you change your spending habits.

Cash is king!

One day as I went to lunch, I met Steve and Sandy in my reception area. They came by to say thanks. What for? This young couple in their twenties had been listening to our radio program, and because I constantly push people to get the right kinds of insurance, they did. Earlier that year they got term life insurance and a medical savings account health-insurance policy (now known as a health savings account, or HSA). "Good thing we did what you said to do," said Steve as he pulled off his cap to reveal a shaved head with a big scar across the top. "What in the world happened?" I asked. The scar was from a biopsy that revealed inoperable brain cancer. Sandy smiled and said, "The health insurance has already paid over $100,000 in bills, and we would be sunk if we hadn't followed through as you push all the time." Also, Steve was uninsurable, so he was thankful to have his term life insurance in place. Steve and Sandy became friends of mine over the next few years as he fought cancer. A friend of mine heard their story and gave them a seven-day Caribbean cruise. Steve lost his battle to cancer in 2005, and we buried him on the day his son was born. He would be proud if his story inspires you to get and keep the right kinds of insurance. He was a good husband and father. By being responsible and buying the right kinds of insurance, they had covered life and death, which we all have to do.

Two years ago, my wife and I were just an average family making the typical financial mistakes most "normal" families do. We believed all the money myths people kept telling us. However, once our mistakes started adding up, they began to really take their toll on us. It wasn't until we stumbled upon Dave's radio show and the Total Money Makeover that we put a stop to our financial foolishness.

Years ago we were not handling our finances well at all. At one point we were married with no kids, making more than $80,000 a year, and we did not have the cash to buy a washing machine. We went along with too many "buy now, pay later" deals. "Ninety days same as cash" sounded like a good idea at the time. WRONG! We ended up paying much more than the items were worth. When we make purchases today, we "buy now, pay now," with $1,800 buying $2,000 worth of furniture.

Another big mistake we made was our life insurance plan. People warned us that we needed to have whole life insurance before we turn thirty "or else." They talked about how amazing the cash value savings feature was. WRONG! We were ignorant about how overpriced the coverage was, how high the fees were, and how long it really took to build cash value. We now know better. We plan to save, invest, and become self-insured.

In 2006, we were still making minimum payments on student loans that we had for more than a decade. We bought into what all the "normal" people were telling us: "Student loans are good debt. Everyone has them." WRONG! We knew we needed to kick Sallie Mae to the curb once and for all. Now, instead of writing her a check every month, we are able to save in advance for our children's college fund.

Fast-forward through the *Financial Peace University* Home Study Kit and fifteen months of complete sacrifice—we've paid off $27,000 in debt, saved an emergency fund, dumped the whole life insurance and purchased term life, created wills, and saved cash for a two-week "Freedom!" beach vacation to celebrate. After a lot of hard work and gazelle intensity, we are finally living like no one else!

**Travis (age 33) and
Merry (age 35) Skinner**
*AutoCAD Draftsman in Land
Surveying; Registered Nurse*

We all hate insurance, until we need it. We pay and pay and pay premiums, and sometimes we feel insurance-poor. There are certainly many gimmicks in the world of insurance. We cover insurance in detail at *Financial Peace University* and in other books, but you must have insurance in some basic categories as part of a Total Money Makeover:

- Auto and Homeowner Insurance—Choose higher deductibles in order to save on premiums. With high liability limits, these are the best buys in the insurance world.
- Life Insurance—Purchase twenty-year level term insurance equal to ten to twelve times your income. Term insurance is cheap and the only way to go; never use life insurance as a place to save money.

- Long-Term Disability—If you are twenty years old, you are about twice as likely to become disabled than to die by age sixty-five. The best place to buy disability insurance is through work at a fraction of the cost. You can usually get coverage that equals from 50 to 70 percent of your income.

- Health Insurance—The number-one cause of bankruptcy today is medical bills. One way to control costs is to look for large deductibles to lower your premium. The health savings account is a great way to save on premiums. The high deductible creates a much lower premium, and this plan allows you to save for medical expenses in a tax-free savings account.

- Long-Term Care Insurance—If you are over sixty, buy long-term care insurance to cover in-home care or nursing home care. The average private nursing home room costs nearly $110,000 per year, which will crack and scramble a nest egg in a heartbeat. Dad in the nursing home can use up Mom's $250,000 savings in just a couple of short years. Make your parents get it.

I was so impressed with Dave when I heard him for the first time on the *Oprah Winfrey Show*. I knew the personal responsibility and financial accountability he was challenging people with were exactly what Ken and I needed. Our financial problems had been accumulating for twenty years and were pretty substantial.

It all started the year after Ken and I were married. He was thirty-one and I was twenty-two—excited about life and the future ahead of us. But everything changed when Ken suffered a severe stroke and was left a quadriplegic. We didn't know what to do (in many regards). Financially, we started putting everything on the credit card because we weren't bringing in much money. Thankfully Ken's medical bills were covered. Without that coverage, the medical bills would have been too much to handle.

For years we racked up debt and were struggling to get by. Nevertheless, God truly blessed us and continued to pull us through everything.

And then we found Dave. Ken and I read *The Total Money Makeover* and began to practice the principles immediately. When we started budgeting, Ken really showed interest in helping me handle our finances and started paying the bills online. The first time that I didn't have to pay the bills, I actually sat down and cried because it was one thing that I didn't have to worry about. Ken lit up, knowing that he was an active partner, making my life a little easier. We have made budgeting and planning our future together enjoyable and fun. It's like dating again! Ken is the most amazing man I have ever met and has been my rock all these years. I am so blessed to be on this journey with him.

**Cheryl (age 44) and
Ken (age 52) Rhoads**

Mary Kay Independent Sales Director

MYTH: If I do a will, I might die.

TRUTH: You are going to die—so do it with a will.

According to CNBC, 67 percent of Americans are set to die without a will. Dumb, really dumb. The state, known for its financial prowess, will decide what happens to your stuff, your kids, and your financial legacy. The proverb says, "A good man leaves an inheritance to his children's children" (Prov. 13:22 NKJV). I am a pragmatist, and so I don't understand all the fretting over a will. A will is a gift you leave your family or loved ones. It is a gift because it makes the management of your estate very clear and light-years easier.

You are going to die, so go out in style, and die with a will in place.

We've revealed debt myths and money myths. If you have carefully read and understood why these myths are untrue, I have great news for you. Your Total Money Makeover has already begun! The Total Money Makeover is a remaking of your view of money so that you permanently change how you deal with money. You must walk to the beat of a different drummer, the same beat that the wealthy hear. If the beat sounds common or normal, evacuate the dance floor immediately. The goal is not to be normal because, as my radio listeners know by now, normal is broke.

5

Two More Hurdles: Ignorance and Keeping Up with the Joneses

Denial (I don't have a problem), debt myths (debt is how you become wealthy), and money myths (stories told by the culture) are three major obstacles that keep you from becoming a fiscally fit body of money management and staying power. Before we move to the proven plan, we must explore two more enemies of your Total Money Makeover.

If you have a major issue with Ben and Jerry's ice cream, you should tell your trainer before you try to change your diet and exercise program. First, you must admit your ice-cream problem and recognize the myths about ice cream as a great weight-loss product. The point is, we must identify the enemy, the hurdles to winning. To set out a game plan and not acknowledge the obstacles to that plan would be immature and unrealistic. Those of us who have been knocked around by life know that we must find the problems or obstacles and plan a way over them, through them, or around them. If you can box up the things that would defeat your Total Money Makeover, then the plan will work. The first step to losing weight and toning up is to identify weight-loss myths, overeating, wrong eating, and no exercise as problems to overcome; the same is true for a Total

Money Makeover. As the great philosopher Pogo from the Sunday comics said years ago, "We have met the enemy and he is us."

Hurdle #1: Ignorance: No One Is Born Financially Smart

The first hurdle is ignorance. In a culture that worships knowledge, to say ignorance about money is an issue makes some people defensive. Don't be defensive. Ignorance is not lack of intelligence; it is lack of know-how. I have seen many newborn babies of friends, relatives, church members, and team members. I have never seen a baby who was born ready to be wealthy. Never do the friends and relatives gather around the window of the nursery and exclaim, "Oh, look! She is a born financial genius!"

No one is born with the knowledge of how to drive a car. We are taught the skill (although some of us don't seem to have learned). No one is born with the knowledge of how to read and write; we are taught how. None of these are innate skills; all must be taught. Likewise, no one is born with the knowledge of how to handle money, but we AREN'T taught that!

At the coffeepot one day, one of my leaders said, "We need to get this Total Money Makeover process taught in college." Before she could graduate from a small Christian college, she was required to take a class on how to interview and hunt for a job. She said the class wasn't very hard academically, but its practical implications made it one of the most valuable classes she took in college. We go to school to learn to earn; we earn and then have no idea what to do with the money. According to the Census Bureau, the median household income in America is right around $75,000. Even if they never get a raise, the average family will make over $3 million in a working lifetime! And we teach NOTHING about how to manage this money in most high schools and colleges. We graduate from school, go out into the world, and get a financial master's degree in D.U.M.B.

Do we make a mess of our finances because we aren't intelligent? No. If you put someone who has never driven a car, has never seen a car, and can't spell *car* in the driver's seat of a brand-new car, the wreck will come before leaving the driveway. Backing up and gaining more speed only leads to another wreck. "Trying harder" isn't the answer because the next wreck will not only total the car but also hurt other people. This is ludicrous!

During our lifetimes Americans average almost $3 million, yet we graduate from high school, college, or even graduate school and can't spell *financial*. This is a bad plan! We have quit teaching personal finance, and we have to start again. That is why "Foundations in Personal Finance" is taught in high schools around the nation; however, our high school curriculum won't help you unless you are still in high school.

If you made a mess of your money and/or haven't gotten the best use from it, usually the reason is that you were never taught to do so. Remember, ignorance doesn't mean dumb; it means you have to learn how. I'm fairly intelligent. I have had multiple best-selling books, speak to millions on my radio and TV programs, and run a multimillion-dollar company, but if you asked me to work on your car, I would make a mess. I don't know how; I'm ignorant in that area.

Overcoming ignorance is easy. First, with no shame, admit that you are not a financial expert because you were never taught. Second, finish this book. Third, go on a lifetime quest to learn more about money. You don't need to apply to Harvard to get an MBA with a specialization in finance; you don't have to watch the financial channel instead of a great movie. You do need to read something about money at least once a year. You should occasionally attend a seminar about money. Your actions should show that you care about money by learning something about it.

Sharon and I have a great marriage—not perfect, but great. Why? We read about marriage, we go to marriage retreat weekends, we date weekly, we sometimes take a Sunday school class on marriage, and we even meet once in a while with a friend who is a Christian marriage counselor. Do we do all these things because our marriage is weak? No, we do all these things to make our marriage great. We have a great marriage because we work at it, make it a priority, and seek knowledge on marriage. Great marriages don't just happen. Wealth doesn't just happen. You will spend some time and effort on getting rid of ignorance. Again, you do not need to become a financial geek; you just need to spend more time on your 401(k) options and your budget than you do picking out this year's vacation.

We were going through life like, as Dave says, "Gomer Pyle on Valium." We didn't have a clue where our money was going. My wife and I couldn't seem to agree on how to manage our incomes. Like all "normal" couples, we thought you HAD to have credit cards to build up your credit and that the SMART thing to do was finance everything. What a huge lie!

Then one day my wife happened to catch *The Ramsey Show*. After listening for a while, she began to share with me the principles Dave talked about, and we were hooked!

The first step in our Total Money Makeover was to get our budget together, which certainly helped us to get organized with our money, but it was also our desire to live a debt-free lifestyle that allowed us to succeed. Next we had to work toward saving for an emergency fund and paying off our debts using the debt snowball.

Baby Step Three (save three to six months of expenses in a fully funded emergency fund), was the hardest step for us. We had to resist the urge to go spend all this available extra money after finishing our debt snowball. Thankfully we built up our emergency fund, because later I lost my job. With no debt and an emergency fund in place, I was able to take my time to find the great job I have today.

Our family life has totally changed for the better. We know what our goals are for our money, and our kids are learning to give, save, and spend money wisely. This plan has helped us regain the hope of financial security and the spiritual peace we all look for in life.

**Walter (age 47) and
Stephanie (age 45) Frick**
Sales Representative; Kindergarten Teacher's Assistant

Ignorance is not okay. "What you don't know won't hurt you" is a really stupid statement. What you don't know will kill you. What you don't know about money will make you broke and keep you broke. Finish this book and read others. You can always check our website at ramsey-solutions.com/store/books for recommended reading by authors generally lined up with our teachings.

Hurdle #2: Keeping Up with the Joneses: The Joneses Can't Do Math

The second hurdle in this chapter is keeping up with the Joneses. Peer pressure, cultural expectations, "reasonable standard of living"—I don't care how you say it, we all need to be accepted by our crowd and our families. This need for approval and respect drives us to do some really insane things. One of the paradoxically dumb things we do is to destroy our finances by buying garbage we can't afford to try to make ourselves appear wealthy to others. Dr. Tom Stanley wrote a wonderful book in the '90s that you should read entitled *The Millionaire Next Door*. His book is a study of America's millionaires. Remember, if you want to be thin and muscular, you should study the habits of people who are thin and muscular. If you want to be rich, you should study the habits and value systems of the rich. In his study of millionaires, Stanley discovered that their habits and value systems were not what most people think. When we think of millionaires, we think of big houses, new cars, and really nice clothes. Stanley found that most millionaires don't have those things. He found the typical millionaire lives in a middle-class home, drives a two-year-old or older paid-for car, and buys blue jeans at Walmart. In short, Stanley found that the typical millionaire found infinitely more motivation from the goal of financial security than from what friends and family thought. The need for approval and respect from others based on what they owned was virtually nonexistent.

If we look at Stanley's findings and hold those up against Ken and

Barbie's life plan, we find Ken and Barbie to be lost, off course, and clueless. Ken and Barbie are in our office all the time for financial counseling. Last year they were here, and their names were Bob and Sara. Bob and Sara make $93,000 per year and have for the last seven years. What do they have to show for it? A $400,000 home that they still owe $390,000 on, including a home equity loan used to furnish it. They have two $30,000 fleeced cars and $52,000 in credit-card debt, but they have traveled well and dressed in high fashion. The $25,000 left on a student loan from college ten years ago is still outstanding because they have no money. On the positive side, they have $2,000 in savings and $18,000 in their 401(k). These people have a negative net worth, but they really look good. Bob's mom is very impressed, and Sara's brother frequently stops by to ask for money because they are "obviously doing well." They present the perfect picture of the American dream that has turned into a nightmare. Behind the perfect hair and the French manicure, there was deep desperation, a sense of futility, an unraveling marriage, and disgust with themselves.

This may be one of the places our metaphor of weight loss for fiscal fitness breaks down. If your body were in the same condition that Bob and Sara's money is in, everyone would think, *Five hundred pounds is just too fat.* Your problem would be apparent to family, friends, strangers, and even you. The difference with Bob and Sara is that they have a "dirty little secret." The secret is that they are nowhere near as cool as they appear. They are broke and desperate, and no one knows it. Not only does no one know it, but everyone thinks the opposite is true. So when my counselor made suggestions to turn around this bankruptcy looking for a place to happen, there was more than one place of resistance in the heart. The truth is that Bob and Sara are broke. They need to get rid of the cars and sell the house.

Resistance of the heart is real. First, of course, we like our nice houses and nice cars, and selling them would be painful. Second, we don't want to admit to everyone we have impressed that we are fakes. Yes, when you buy a big pile of stuff with no money and lots of debt, you are a financial fake. Peer pressure is very, very powerful. "We are scaling down" is a painful statement to make to friends or family. "We will have to pass on that trip or dinner because it is not in our budget" is virtually impossible for some people to say. Being real takes tremendous courage. We like approval, and we like respect, and to say otherwise is another form of denial. To wish for the admiration of others is normal. The problem is that this admiration can become a drug. Many of you are addicted to this drug, and the destruction to your wealth and financial well-being caused by your addiction is huge.

Radical change in the quest for approval, which has involved purchasing stuff with money we don't have, is required for a money breakthrough. Sara's breakthrough came with family. Her family was upper-middle-crust and had always given Christmas gifts to every member. With twenty nieces and nephews and six sets of adults to buy for, just on her side, the budget was ridiculous. Sara's announcement at Thanksgiving that this year Christmas giving was going to be done with the drawing of names, because she and Bob couldn't afford it, was earth-shattering. Some of you are grinning as if this is no big deal. It was a huge deal in Sara's family! Gift giving was a tradition! Her mother and two of her sisters-in-law were furious. Very little thanks were given that Thanksgiving, but Sara stood her ground and said, "No more."

Sara has a master's degree in sociology, so she is no pushover. She understood how the family dynamic would be upset, and she understood that she would lose approval, admiration, and respect. Sara said later that while she grasped intellectually what her announcement meant, and she knew emotionally and financially that this was the correct thing to do, the reality was very hard. Strong peer pressure from her family literally kept her awake the whole night before. She told me, "As I lay in the dark, I was afraid, like a little twelve-year-old girl yearning for approval from her daddy." The courage to address what may seem like a small issue was a huge breakthrough for Sara. That Thanksgiving her heart had a Total

Money Makeover, and she was not going to be led into well-dressed poverty by peer pressure anymore.

Our financial makeover began in March 2008, when we bought a copy of *The Total Money Makeover* while on vacation. I read the foreword aloud to my husband as we drove home, and he asked me to continue reading. Four hours later, my voice was hoarse and tired, but we were still reading as the family minivan pulled into the driveway! We were hooked and energized. It felt like our whole world had just been lit up!

That same night, we pulled out all of our bills and made a list of everything we owed. Then, we made a budget. It took hours, but afterward we were ready to attack our debt! We set a goal to pay everything off in time to celebrate some major milestones that were less than a year away: our fifteenth wedding anniversary and Darrin's fortieth birthday. At the time, it seemed impossible!

We've always had car payments and credit-card payments—there's never been a time when we were debt-free. We avoided discussing money because it would always end with an argument or someone's feelings getting hurt. We simply pretended our personal finances didn't exist.

But with our new plan in place, we went crazy and never looked back. We cut up our credit cards one by one as we paid them off. More important, we got on the same page with our money, which is something we never thought possible!

In ten months we paid off $58,000 of debt and put $18,000 toward our fully funded emergency fund! We're teaching our three boys how to save their money and make smart decisions with it. They've learned about the dangers of credit cards and how to compare prices on things they want.

Not only are we confident about our financial future today, but we are more excited about it than any other time in our lives. Words can't describe the burden that has been lifted from our hearts and minds! We've really had a Total Money Makeover!

Kristin (age 39) and
Darrin (age 40) Schmidt
Stay-at-Home Mom; Accountant

Everyone has a weak spot like Sara's. It could be your third-generation failing business that needs to be closed. It could be your clothes shopping. It probably is your car. It could be the boat. Maybe yours is giving to your grown children. Unless you have had a heart-level Total Money Makeover somewhere, sometime in your life, you are still doing something with money to impress others, and that has to change before you can get on a real plan to fiscal fitness. The Bible states, "Godliness with contentment is great gain" (1 Tim. 6:6 NKJV). Those of us who have had a Total Money Makeover still know where our Achilles' heel is and still see that weak spot as a fatal wound if we allow it to grow again. What is the one "money thing" that makes you grin inside when you see others admiring it? Do you need to give it up to break that feeling inside you? Until you recognize that weak area, you will always be prone to financial stupidity on that subject.

My weak spot is cars. After starting with nothing and becoming a millionaire the first time by age twenty-six, I had the eye of my heart set on a Jaguar. I "needed" a Jaguar. What I needed was for people to be impressed with my success. What I needed was my family raising an eyebrow of approval based on my ability to win. What I yearned for was respect. What I was so shallow to believe was that the car I drove gave me those things. God used the whole story of what I drove to give my heart a Total Money Makeover in the area of peer pressure.

Totally Broke and Driving a Jag!

As I was going broke, losing everything, I kept the Jaguar by refinancing it repeatedly at different, friendlier banks. I even went so far as to get a good friend to cosign a loan so I could keep this image car. I couldn't afford to keep up the maintenance on the car, so it began to deteriorate. It ran poorly and wasn't reliable, but I still loved it and hung on. Within the year of our bankruptcy, we were so broke that our electricity was once cut off for two days. I have often wondered what the guy from the electric company thought as he stood in the driveway next to my Jaguar and pulled my electric meter. That is sick. The car continued to deteriorate, and the main seal on the oil pan cracked. This caused oil coming out the back of the engine onto the muffler to burn. The burning oil, lots of it, created a smoke screen for miles behind me everywhere I went. The bid to fix it was $1,700, and I hadn't seen an extra $1,700 in months, so I just kept driving my James Bond smoke-screen mobile. Finally, my friend got really tired of making the payments he had cosigned for and gently suggested I sell my precious car. I was mad at him. How dare he suggest that I sell my car! So he quit making the payments, and the bank not so gently suggested I sell the car or they would repo it. I tried to stall and only came to my senses and sold the Jaguar on a Thursday morning because the bank assured me they would take it on Friday. I was able to work my way through the mess, pay the bank and even my friend back, but the process was humiliating. Because I was too stubborn to address what that car represented in my life, I caused much damage that was avoidable.

An interesting footnote about how healing can occur on your weak spot: I was so disgusted with myself when I woke up and realized the depth of my stupidity that I swore off my drug, cars. I went to abstinence, meaning I didn't care what we drove or what it looked like as long as we were winning in our Total Money Makeover. Fast-forward fifteen years. We had become wealthy again, and I decided to get a different car. I'm always looking for a one- or two-year-old car, I'm always paying cash, and I'm always looking for a deal, not really caring what car it is. I was kind of looking for a Mercedes or a Lexus, but I was really looking for a steal. A friend in the car business called me with a deal—on a Jaguar. So all those years and tears later, when it was no longer the driving force of my approval rating, God allowed a Jaguar back into my life. He returned what the locusts had eaten, but He only did so when it was not my idol. Rumor has it that God doesn't like us to have other gods in our lives.

Looking back, we were your typical American family: making good money, having lots of nice toys, and drowning in debt. We always told ourselves we deserved new cars and we needed a house so we could stop paying rent.

A friend at work was talking about Dave Ramsey one day, and it intrigued me, so I got his book *The Total Money Makeover*, and we started reading. We got motivated because we heard the stories of people making much less than us but who were debt-free—a place we wanted to be.

Establishing a budget was priority, but first we had to overcome the mindset that we "needed" stuff to make us happy. We were able to pay off our debt without having to give up too much; instead, we redirected what we already had.

The change has been amazing. My wife no longer feels guilty for spending money on much-needed clothes. I can relax when it comes to paying bills at the end of the month, knowing there's still money in the checking account. It's all worth it.

We now talk about our finances instead of just fighting about money. We have been able to save for retirement and know that if anything happens to one of us, the other is taken care of and will not be burdened with debt.

My wife and I have been debt-free since January of 2004, and life is so much easier now.

**Brian (age 36) and
Tammy (age 33) McKinley**
*Purchasing Agent for Physician Management
Organization; Agricultural Economist*

So maybe someday Sara and Bob will be able to pay cash to take Sara's whole family on a cruise for Christmas. After their Total Money Makeover, Bob and Sara will be able to pay cash for a huge event like that and not even dent their wealth. They will be able to buy that cruise in memory of that fateful Thanksgiving when Sara's heart had a Total Money Makeover in her need for her family's approval. That change has taught Sara and Bob that if they will live like no one else, later they will be able to live like no one else.

Past the Obstacle Course and Up the Mountain

One thing I have learned as I have lost fat, become toned, and generally gotten into better shape is this: things that require physical output are easier for me. Things like mountain climbing or obstacle courses are actually doable now, not a dream as they were when I was overweight and out of shape. The same is true of our Total Money Makeover journey to fiscal fitness. Have you realized by now that the start of your Total Money Makeover is almost an obstacle course? We busted through denial. We waded through and climbed over debt myths. We carefully scaled the wall of money myths. We are working through ignorance. And we have learned not to place so much emphasis on our competition on the course; we have permanently quit keeping up with the Joneses, because the Joneses are broke. The obstacle course, however, was only part of our journey.

Now we stand at the bottom of a mountain with a clear view of the top. We are in better shape now for mountain climbing, and there are no blind spots. We are ready to climb. The goal is far off, but we can see it clearly now. There is a distinct and very clear path we will take to the top. The good thing about this path is that it is not virgin territory; it is a well-worn path. It is a narrow path, one that most people don't follow, but many winners have. Tens of thousands have followed this path once they made it through the obstacle course.

Take a look back before we start. The climb will be hard, but it will be near impossible if you are still struggling with any of the obstacles, if you are still hanging on to myths, denial, or any other obstacles. On this mountain climb you will feel as if you have bricks in your backpack. A couple of pounds of denial might not be fatal, but mixing it with three pounds of "I still think credit cards are good" and a can or two of "folding to peer pressure" will result in a backpack load that will ensure your climb is a failure. Most of us make the first climb wearing a hat of ignorance, and while it will slow the climb, ignorance will not keep anyone from the top when mixed with some humility. This mountain is doable, but not if you are still bogged down on the obstacle course. Some things I'll tell you to do won't work and will cause damage if you still cling to denial, myths, ignorance, or approval.

Decide before the climb if you are going to follow the guide. If you aren't going to listen to the seasoned guide who has personally made this climb alone and then returned to lead tens of thousands up this path, then you climb at your own peril. Finish reading the book even if you don't agree with me, but following these steps while trying to hold on to myths, ignorance, approval, or denial will make your climb very hard and may injure you.

Why not climb? The only other path is to follow all the normal people who are broke. That isn't a path; it is a well-beaten interstate highway. Most people drive around and around, occasionally glancing forlornly at the mountain we will climb, but when they see how tough the obstacle course is just to get to the bottom, those sad souls quit before they ever begin.

The twelve-steppers have it right. They say, "Continuing to do the same thing over and over again and expecting a different result is the definition of insanity." What you have falsely believed and acted on or not acted on has brought you to the place you are today with your money. If you want to be in a different place, you must believe and do things differently. If I want a smaller waist size than fifty-two inches, I must eat and exercise differently. The change will be painful, but the result will be worth it.

I've been to the top of Total Money Makeover Mountain, and I've led countless others there. I say, IT IS WORTH THE EFFORT! So lace up your shoes of resolve, wave goodbye to your "normal" friends, and let's climb!

6

Save $1,000 Fast: Walk Before You Run

Financial Peace University, our flagship personal finance course, revolves around the "Baby Steps," the premise of which is that we can do anything financially if we do it one little step at a time. I have developed the Baby Steps over years of counseling one-on-one, in small-group discussions, with real-world lives in *Financial Peace University* and by answering questions on our radio show. Tens of thousands have followed this tried-and-true system to achieve their Total Money Makeover. The term *Baby Steps* comes from the 1991 comedy film *What About Bob?* starring Bill Murray. Bill plays a crazy guy who drives his psychiatrist crazy. The therapist, played by Richard Dreyfuss, has written a book called *Baby Steps*. The statement "You can get anywhere if you simply go one step at a time" is the framework for the movie. We will use the Baby Steps to walk through our Total Money Makeover. Why do the Baby Steps work? I thought you would never ask.

Eating an Elephant Gives You Energy

The way you eat an elephant is one bite at a time. Find something to do and do that with vigor until it is complete; then and only then do you move to the next step. If you try to do everything at once, you will fail. If you woke up this morning and realized you needed to lose one hundred pounds, build your cardiovascular system, and tone your muscles, what would you do? If on the first day of your new plan you quit eating, run three miles, and lift all the weight you can lift with every muscle group, you will collapse. If you don't collapse the first day, wait forty-eight hours for the muscle groups to lock up and the cardio to go crazy, and you will be bingeing on food shortly thereafter. When I went on a quest for a better body and better health a few years ago, my wise trainer didn't try to kill me the first day. Not even by the second week were we pushing the envelope, because he knew I had to create some muscle tone before we could hit hard workouts. We walked before we ran. Plus, if I had tried to do everything at once, I would have been overwhelmed and frustrated with my inability to do it all.

The power of focus is what causes our Baby Steps to work. When you try to do everything at once, progress can be very slow. When you put 3 percent in your 401(k), $50 extra on the house payment, and $5 extra on the credit card, you dilute your efforts. Because you attack several areas at once, you don't *finish* anything you start for a long time. That makes you feel that you aren't accomplishing anything, which is very dangerous. If you feel that nothing is getting done, you will soon lose energy for the task of money management altogether. The power of focus is that it works. Things happen. You check stuff off your list. Life gives you an "attaboy" in the form of actual visible progress.

The power of priority also causes the Baby Steps to work. Each of these steps is part of the proven plan to financial fitness I promised you. They build on one another; therefore, if done out of order, they do not work. Think of a 350-pound person beginning marathon training with a quick ten-mile run. The results of not building up to that run could be total frustration at best and a heart attack at worst. So do the Baby Steps in order. Walk around the block and lose some weight before going on a ten-mile run.

To start the Baby Steps, we will work on one important step to the exclusion of others. Patience! We will climb the whole mountain, but not until we first have a strong base camp. You will be tempted to short-circuit the process because you are more concerned about one certain area of your money, but don't do it. These steps are the proven plan to financial fitness, and they are in the right order for everyone. For example, if you are fifty-five with no retirement, you may be tempted to jump to Step Four (invest 15 percent of your income in retirement), because you are scared about not being able to retire with dignity. The paradox is that by shortcutting the process, you are much more likely to fail at retiring with dignity. Failure could also occur when you cash out your newly formed retirement plan to cover the inevitable emergency. If you have kids heading toward college, you may be panicking about saving for college, which is covered in Baby Step Five (save for your children's college fund), but don't do it out of order. I will address the problems you'll run into at each stage if you get things out of order, because I have seen most of them. Focus exclusively on the Baby Step you are on, even though it seems to be a temporary detriment to other areas of money. Things will be fine if you don't focus on retirement for a few months, as long as you can kick retirement into the stratosphere when we get there.

YOU, Inc.

This chapter is about the first Baby Step, but before we discuss saving $1,000 fast, we need to look at some basic tools needed to win and some ongoing things you should be doing as you go. The dreaded *B* word enters the picture here. You must set up a budget, a written budget, every month. This is a book about a process that will enable you to win with your money, a process that others have completed successfully, and I assure you that virtually none of the thousands of winners I have seen did so without a written budget.

We were so motivated to start our Total Money Makeover when we finally realized that what we were doing wasn't working. Every month there was more month than money, and all we would do is fight about it. We were sick and tired of being sick and tired!

Budgeting was the best and the hardest part of the whole process. We needed to make sure we had our money going toward certain debts while cutting back on WANTS. It takes some effort every week and, for sure, discipline, and if we were good at either, we would have never been in this mess.

Our biggest sacrifice has been having to wait. We wait on a lot of things now until we actually have the money. What a great idea! Christmas will be different this year. I think it will be a lot better because everything under the tree will be paid for, and we'll actually enjoy it instead of regret it.

The change is evident in so many areas of our life. We feel comfortable knowing that we will be able to save for our children's college and we're able to tithe consistently. And the funny thing is that we don't miss the money.

Living debt-free has been amazing. My wife and I communicate better, and we're more loving to each other and the kids because we aren't stressed out about money all of the time.

**Tony (age 36) and
Tara (age 37) Kiger**
Small-Business Owner, Homemaker

In chapter four on money myths, the importance of a written budget was discussed. If you worked for a company called YOU, Inc., and your job at YOU, Inc., was to manage money—and you managed money at YOU, Inc., the way you manage your own money now, would YOU, Inc., fire you? You have to tell money what to do or it leaves. A written budget for the month is your money goal. People who win at anything have written goals. Goals are what you are aiming at. Zig Ziglar says, "If you aim at nothing, you will hit it every time." Money won't behave unless you tame it. P. T. Barnum said, "Money is an excellent slave and a horrible master." You wouldn't build a house without a blueprint, so why do you spend your lifetime income of over $3 million without a blueprint? Jesus said, "Which of you, intending to build a tower, does not sit down first and count the cost, whether he has enough to finish it?" (Luke 14:28 NKJV).

There never seemed to be enough "bucks" to cover all our family's expenses. I was panicked each month because we were barely squeaking by: paying our bills, funding extracurricular activities for our kids, paying for car repairs, etc. John was frustrated because his check was gone before he walked in the door. There was too little to go around, and we had huge differences in opinion regarding what to pay first. Thanks to a friend, I ended up reading *The Total Money Makeover* and realized our family's financially peaceful future was just around the corner if we could get everyone onboard.

Sure enough, after John read Dave's book, he came to the same conclusions I had. We were so excited to be on the same page financially and start using our money wisely! We established a budget and got rid of our credit cards. We knew we had to work together to accomplish our goal, so we've spent a lot of time communicating with one another concerning how our spending can really enhance the lives of our family. A lot of couples forfeit working together on their budgets, and one always ends up pushing and nagging the other. It is so important to work with each other from the very beginning! It might seem boring, but we've turned our regular budget/calendar meetings into enjoyable, future-planning dates!

It's so nice not to have anxiety about money. We have been able to do so much more with our four kids and truly enjoy those special times with them. Also, we're making plans to add a second floor to our house. Before starting Dave's plan, I had a hard time dreaming with John about it because I thought it would never happen. Now I can see that second floor in our near future. Making a plan and sticking to it has made all the difference for the entire family. I can't imagine living without a budget! The financial rewards are wonderful, but the peace of mind it has given John and me is even greater.

Sarada (age 34) and
John (age 37) Marsh
Homemaker; Civil Engineer

Brian Tracy, motivational speaker, says, "What does it take to succeed on a big scale? A tremendous God-given talent? Inherited wealth? A decade of postgraduate education? Connections? Fortunately for most of us, what it takes is something very simple and accessible: clear, written goals." A study from Dominican University of California backs him up. It shows that people who write down goals are 42 percent more successful than those who don't!

This is not a textbook on money; this is a book on the steps to take and how to take them. This isn't a chapter on budgeting; however, many of our budget forms from the Financial Peace software program are in the back of this book for you to use. The instructions are on each page, but let me give you a couple of guidelines to get started on budgeting.

Set up a new budget every month. Don't try to have the perfect budget for the perfect month, because we never have those. Spend every dollar on paper before the month begins. Give every dollar of your income a name before the month begins, which is called a zero-based budget. Income minus outgo equals zero every month. Look at this month's income and this month's bills, savings, and debts, and match them up until you have given every income dollar an outgo name. If you have an irregular income due to commissions, self-employment, or bonuses, use the Irregular-Income Planning sheet (go to www.ramseysolutions.com/budgeting/useful-forms) to create a prioritized spending plan, but you still must do a written budget before each month begins. (The EveryDollar app can also help you do this digitally. Scan the QR code at the end of chapter two or chapter seven to get started.)

The financial mentality I grew up with said, "If you want anything out of life, you're going to have to get into debt for it!" And so I did. By the time I was in my mid-twenties, I had accumulated $3,000 in debt on a mobile home, $9,000 in debt on a car, approximately $1,000 on credit cards, and $50,000 on a newly purchased home. That's a lot of debt to pay off on a salary of around $30,000 a year.

It wasn't until my cousin and her husband introduced me to Dave that I began to make a change in how I handled my money. They had attended *Financial Peace University* at a local church and decided to share the CDs with me. A few hours into the CDs, the light came on. I knew that I had to get ahold of my finances and start living life differently. I purchased *Financial Peace* and *The Total Money Makeover* and began listening online to Dave every weekday.

My most important move in becoming financially free: budgeting. I nearly passed out when I realized how much I was spending on eating out! It took a few months to organize my funds and expenses, but now I've become a great budgeter! I give 10 percent of every paycheck, and I'm currently allotting 49 percent of my salary to paying off my house. But thanks to careful budgeting and spending, I'll be able to assign 52 percent of my paycheck to the house at the turn of the year! Then I will be able to give more and help others find the peace that I have found.

Jaime Morgan (age 27)
Agriculture Communications

Agree on It

If you're married, agree on the budget with your spouse. This one sentence requires a stand-alone book to describe how, but the bottom line is this: if you aren't working together, it is almost impossible to win. Once the budget is agreed on and is in writing, pinkie-swear and spit-shake that you will never do anything with money that is not on that paper. The paper is the boss of the money, and you are the boss of what goes on the paper, but you have to stick to the budget, or it's just an elaborate theory.

If something comes up in the middle of the month that causes the budget to need changing, call an emergency budget committee meeting. You can change the budget (and what you do with money) only if you do two things. One, both spouses agree to the change. Two, you must still balance your budget. If you increase what you are spending on car repairs by $50, you must lower what you are spending somewhere else by $50 so that your income minus your outgo still equals zero. This process of midcourse adjustment doesn't have to be a big hairy deal, but both guidelines must be met. You still zero out so you don't blow the budget, and you get spousal approval so you haven't broken the spit pact.

Adriaaaan!

Before we get to Baby Step One, you will have to do one other thing. You will have to be current with all your creditors. If you are behind on payments, the first goal will be to become current. If you are far behind, do necessities first, which are basic food, shelter, utilities, clothing, and transportation. Only when you're current with the necessities can you catch up on credit cards and student loans. If you need more help with this level of crisis, check our website (ramseysolutions.com) for how to contact one of our Ramsey Preferred financial coaches.

DAVE RANTS . . .

The number-one cause of divorce in America is money fights and money problems. Spouses just don't know how to talk to each other about money. That's because most of the time the husband and wife have totally different personalities about every-thing—and that includes their money.

In every marriage, there's what I call the Nerd and the Free Spirit. The Nerd has fun with numbers and feels like it gives them control. They feel like they are taking care of their loved ones.

But the Free Spirit doesn't feel cared for; they feel controlled! They don't want anything to do with the numbers, and they tend to "forget" about the budget.

Guess what? Neither the Nerd nor the Free Spirit is "right" or "wrong." You're a team! You need to have a plan, but you need to have some fun. You need to save, but you need to spend a little. The trick is to figure out how your differences can comple-ment each other, and then you can work together.

That only happens when you both sit down together and make a plan. The Nerd can write up the first draft of the budget, but the Free Spirit has to sit down and look at it. Heck, I even make the Free Spirit *change* something on the budget! That freaks out the Nerds, but this is supposed to be "our" plan, right? That means both spouses need to have mature input and shared goals.

Larry Burkett used to say that if two people just alike get married, one of you is unnecessary. You and your spouse are different, so celebrate the differences and learn to work together on this money stuff!

Focused intensity is required to win. I can't stress enough that people who have had a Total Money Makeover, those noted in this book and others across America, got mad. They got sick and tired of being sick and tired! They said, "We've had it!" and went ballistic to change their lives. There is no intellectual exercise where you can academically work your way into wealth; you have to get fired up. Play the music from *Rocky* in the background and listen for Rocky's cry: "Adriaaaan!" Go get 'em, champ! There is no energy in logic; this is behavior and motivation modification, and it works!

After you are current; have a written, agreed-on plan; have the obstacle course behind you; and are focused and intense, you are ready to follow the right priorities. Here we go.

Baby Step One: Save $1,000 Cash for Your Starter Emergency Fund

It is going to rain. You need a rainy day fund. You need an umbrella. *Money* magazine says that 78 percent of us will have a major negative event in a given ten-year period of time. The job is downsized, right-sized, reorganized, or you just plain get fired. There's an unexpected pregnancy: "We weren't going to have kids yet/another one." Car blows up. Transmission goes out. You bury a loved one. Grown kids move home again. Life happens, so be ready. This is not a surprise. You need an emergency fund, an old-fashioned Grandma's rainy day fund. Sometimes people tell me I should be more positive. Well, I *am* positive; it *is* going to rain, so you need a rainy day fund. Now, obviously, $1,000 isn't going to catch all these big things, but it will catch the little ones until the emergency fund is fully funded.

We don't have and never will have credit cards ever again. "Why?" you might ask (at least a lot of our family and friends do). Because we have found security and trust in God for the provision of all our needs, and we have gained the strength to build up an emergency fund that can handle sudden expenses we weren't expecting. Most people use the excuse that you should have at least one credit card for emergencies. We have found a much better strategy. Plan ahead and build an emergency fund that can cover (with cash) whatever might come up.

We have learned that getting a hold on your attitude is the number-one factor in being victorious over your finances. We now tell the money where to go instead of it guiding us around and enslaving us to others (such as student loans and credit-card companies). In gaining a newfound respect and understanding of what we have been given, we have come to acknowledge and take responsibility for the money God has blessed us with. We had to face our debt and our desires and become better stewards of our possessions and income. Before, we didn't realize that every little dollar adds up. The choice we had to make was whether we wanted those growing dollars in our savings account or on our credit-card statements.

Saving that initial $1,000 is so important to the rest of your Total Money Makeover. It teaches you how to prepare for your unknown future and trust that when things do come up, you'll be able to handle them. It was so much easier to attack our debt and get rid of our credit cards knowing that we had some money in the bank to cover our backs if something came up. We don't have to have a false sense of security in our credit cards anymore. We've been good stewards and have real security because of our habits and perseverance. Sacrifice has had its place in our budgeting wants and desires, but it is completely worth it. We remind ourselves that delaying a purchase doesn't mean we will never have it. Trusting God, timing, patience, and preparation are everything, though, when it comes to gaining financial peace.

Stacie (age 35) and
André (age 36) Bledsoe
Data Analyst; Production Technician

This emergency fund is not for buying things or for vacation; it is for emergencies only. No cheating. Do you know who Murphy is? Murphy is that guy with all those negative laws, such as, "If it can go wrong, it will." For years I have worked with people who felt that Murphy was a member of their families. They have spent so much time with trouble that they think trouble is a first cousin. Interestingly enough, when we have had a Total Money Makeover, Murphy leaves. A Total Money Makeover is no guarantee of a trouble-free life, but my observation has been that trouble, Murphy, is not as welcome in homes that have an emergency fund. Saving money for emergencies is Murphy repellent! Being broke all the time seems to attract ol' Murphy to set up residence.

Most of America uses credit cards to catch all of life's "emergencies." Some of these so-called emergencies are events like Christmas. Christmas is not an emergency; it doesn't sneak up on you. Christmas is always in December; they don't move it. Therefore it is not an emergency. Your car will need repairs, and your kids will outgrow their clothes. These are not emergencies; they are items that belong in your budget. If you don't budget for them, they will feel like emergencies. Americans use the credit cards to cover actual emergencies too. Things discussed earlier, like job layoffs, are real emergencies and are the reason for an emergency fund. A leather couch on sale is not an emergency.

Whether the emergency is real or just poor planning, the cycle of dependence on credit cards has to be broken. A well-planned budget for anticipated things and an emergency fund for the truly unexpected can end dependence on credit cards.

The first major Baby Step to your Total Money Makeover is to begin the emergency fund. A small start is to save $1,000 in cash *fast*! If you have a household income under $20,000 per year, use $500 for your beginner fund. Those who earn more than $20,000 should get together $1,000 fast! Stop everything and focus.

Since I hate debt so much, people often ask why we don't start with the debt. I used to do that when I first started teaching and counseling, but I discovered that people would stop their whole Total Money Makeover because of an emergency—they felt guilty that they had to stop debt-reducing to survive. It's like stopping your whole fitness program because you get a sore knee from a fall when running; you'll find any excuse will do. The alternator on the car would go out, and that $300 repair ruined the whole plan because the purchase had to go on a credit card since there was no emergency fund. If you use debt after swearing off it, you lose the momentum to keep going. It is like eating seven pounds of ice cream on Friday after losing two pounds that week. You feel sick, like a failure.

So start with a little fund to catch the little things before beginning to dump the debt. It is like drinking a light protein shake to fortify your body so you can work out, which enables you to lose weight. The beginner fund will keep life's little Murphies from turning into new debt while you work off the old debt. If a real emergency happens, you have to handle it with your emergency fund. No more borrowing! You have to break the cycle.

Twist and wring out the budget, work extra hours, sell something, or have a garage sale, but quickly get your $1,000. Most of you should hit this step in less than a month. If it looks as though it is going to take longer, do something radical. Deliver pizzas, work part-time, or sell something else. Get crazy. You are way too close to the edge of falling over a major money cliff here. Remember, if the Joneses (all the broke people) think you are cool, you are heading the wrong way. If they think you are crazy, you are probably on track.

Hide It

When you get the $1,000, hide it. You can't keep the money handy because it will get spent. If your $1,000 from Baby Step One is in the underwear drawer, the pizza man will get it. No, the pizza man isn't in your underwear drawer, but you will impulse-buy something if the money is easily accessible. You can put it in the bank savings account, but it cannot become overdraft protection. Don't attach the savings account to your checking to protect you from overdrafting because then your emergency fund will get spent on impulse. I have had to learn to protect myself from me. We are not putting the money in the bank to earn money, but rather to make it hard to get. Since $1,000 at 4 percent earns only $40 per year, you aren't getting rich here, just finding a safe place to park money.

Get creative. Maria, who attended one of our classes, went to her local Walmart and bought a cheap 8" x 10" frame. She framed ten $100 bills in a stack. In the space within the frame she wrote, "In case of emergency, break glass." Then she hung the emergency fund on the wall behind coats in a closet. She knew the average burglar wouldn't look there, and it would be too much trouble for her to get it out of the closet and out of the frame, so she wouldn't use it unless there was an emergency. Whether you use a simple savings account or a frame in the coat closet, get your $1,000 quickly.

Keep It Liquid

This is a small step, so take it quickly! Don't let this small first step last for months! What if you already have more than $1,000? Wow, that was easy, wasn't it? If you already have the $1,000 in anything other than retirement plans, get it out. If it is in a certificate of deposit with penalties, take the penalty for early withdrawal and get it out. If it is in mutual funds, get it out. If it is in savings bonds, get it out. If it is in checking, get it out. If it is in stocks or bonds, get it out. Your emergency fund, limited to $1,000 in liquid, available cash, is all that is acceptable. If you have tried to get fancy with the emergency fund, you are likely to borrow to keep from "cashing it (the cool investment) out." Details will come later in *The Total Money Makeover* about what to do with your fully funded emergency fund.

All money you have above and beyond the $1,000 in anything except retirement plans will be used in the next step anyway, so get ready. You won't have this money to fall back on if the alternator on your car goes out.

What if you are at Baby Step Two (Pay Off All Debt (Except the House) Using the Debt Snowball) in the next chapter and you use $300 from your emergency fund to fix the alternator? If this happens, stop Step Two and return to Step One until the full $1,000 is replenished. Once your beginner emergency fund is funded again, you can return to Step Two. Otherwise, you will gradually do away with this small buffer and be back to old habits of borrowing to cover real emergencies.

I know some of you think this step is very simplistic. For some this is an instantaneous step, and for others this is the first time they have ever had enough control over their money to save it. For some readers, this is an easy step. For others, this is the step that will be the spiritual and emotional basis for the entire Total Money Makeover.

Lilly was such a case. A single mom with two kids, she had been divorced for eight years; struggle had been a way of life for some time. Lilly had survival debt, not stupid, spoiled-brat debt. She had been ripped off with a super-high-interest car loan, check-advance debt, and lots of credit-card debt. She had a take-home pay of only $1,200 per month with two baby birds to feed, along with a host of greedy rip-off lenders. Saving seemed like such a fairy tale to her that she had long ago lost hope of ever being able to save money. When I met her she had already begun her Total Money Makeover. After hearing me teach the Baby Steps at a live event, weeks later she dropped by a book signing to give me an unsolicited report.

As she moved through the book line, I looked up and saw a huge grin. She asked if she could give me a big hug to say thanks. How could I turn that down? As I looked at her, tears began to run down her cheeks as she gleefully told of fighting through a budget, her first ever. She told me of years of struggle. Then she laughed, and everyone in line (now fully engaged) cheered when she said she now has $500 in cash saved. This was the first $500 in her adult life that was earmarked for her emergency fund. This was the first time she had had money between her and Murphy. Her friend, Amy, who was with Lilly that day, told me that Lilly was a different person already. Amy said, "Even her face has changed, now that she has peace." Don't be confused; it wasn't $500 that did all that. What caused Lilly's liberation was her newfound hope. She had hope that she never had before. She had hope because she had a sense of power and control over money. Money had been an enemy her whole life, and now that she had tamed it, money was going to be Lilly's new lifelong companion.

How about you? Now is the time to decide. Is this theory, or is it real?

Am I a simpleton kook, or have I found something that works? Keep reading, and we will decide together.

Scan this QR code for thirty easy ways you can save up to $1,000 for your starter emergency fund—fast.

7

The Debt Snowball: Lose Weight Fast, Really

Your Total Money Makeover is dependent upon using your most powerful tools. I believe with everything within me that your most powerful wealth-building tool is your income. Ideas, strategies, goals, vision, focus, and even creative thinking are vastly important, but until you get control and full use of your income to build wealth, you will not build and keep wealth. Some of you might inherit money or win a jackpot, but that is dumb luck, not a proven plan to financial fitness. To build wealth, YOU will have to regain control of your income.

Identify the Enemy

The bottom line is that it is easy to become wealthy if you don't have any payments. You may get sick of hearing it, but the key to winning any battle is to identify the enemy. The reason I am so passionate about your getting rid of debt is that I have seen how many people make huge strides toward being a millionaire in the short time after they get rid of their payments. If you didn't have a car payment, a student loan, credit cards out your ears, medical debt, or even a mortgage, you could become wealthy very quickly. I know that may seem like a faraway place for some of you. You might feel like a 350-pounder looking at Mr. Universe, shaking your head, thinking it will never happen for you. Let me assure you, I have walked with many 350-pounders into financial fitness, so stay with me.

The math is revealing. The typical American household with a $75,000 annual income would normally have a $1,970 house payment and a $560 car payment. Then there is a $250 student-loan payment; and the average credit-card debt is about $11,000, making those monthly payments around $275 per month. Also, this typical household will have other miscellaneous debt on things like furniture, electronics, or personal loans on which they pay an additional $120. All these payments total $3,175 per month. If this family were to invest that instead of sending it to the creditors, they would be cash mutual-fund millionaires in just thirteen years! (After thirteen years, it gets really exciting. They'll have $2 million in five more years, $3 million in three more years, $4 million in two and a half more years, and $5 million in two more years. So they will have $5 million after twenty-five years.) Keep in mind, this is with an average income, which means many of you make more than this! If you are thinking that you don't have that many payments so your math won't work, you missed the point. If you make $75,000 and have fewer payments, you have a head start, since you already have more control of your income than most people.

With a take-home pay of $5,000, could you invest $3,175 if you had no payments? All you have to pay for are utilities, food, clothes, insurance, and other miscellaneous expenses. That would be tight, but doable. If you do that for just thirteen years, you will have a pinnacle experience. I will explain that later.

Many of you reading this are convinced that you could become wealthy if you could get out of debt. The problem now is that you are feeling more and more trapped by the debt. I have great news! I have a foolproof, but very difficult, method for getting out of debt. Most people won't do it because they are average, but not you. You have already figured out that if you will live like no one else, later you can live like no one else. You are sick and tired of being sick and tired, so you are willing to pay the price for greatness. This is the toughest of all the Baby Steps to your Total Money Makeover. It is so hard, but it is so worth it. This step requires the most effort, the most sacrifice, and is where all your broke friends and relatives will make fun of you (or join you). This step requires you to shave your head and drink the Kool-Aid. Just kidding, but not by much. Your focused intensity has to go off the scale. Remember the Albert Einstein quote from earlier in the book? "Great spirits have often encountered violent opposition from weak minds."

If you really believe that wealth building will no longer be a dream but a reality if you have no payments, you should be willing to do bizarre and sacrificial things to have no payments. Time to pay off the DEBT!

Baby Step Two: Pay Off All Debt (Except the House) Using the Debt Snowball

The way we pay off the debt is called the debt snowball. The debt snowball forms, as well as the budget forms, are in the back of the book and are available on our website: ramseysolutions.com/budgeting/useful-forms. We also have a handy debt snowball calculator: ramseysolutions.com/debt/debt-calculator. The debt snowball process is simple to understand but will require truckloads of effort. Remember what my pastor said: "It isn't complicated, but it is difficult." We have discussed that personal finance is 80 percent behavior and 20 percent head knowledge. The debt snowball is designed the way it is because we are more concerned with modifying behavior than correct mathematics. (You'll see what I mean shortly.) Being a certified nerd, I always used to start with making the math work. I have learned that the math does need to work, but sometimes motivation is more important than math. This is one of those times.

The debt snowball method requires you to list all your debts in order of smallest payoff balance to largest. List all your debts except your home;

we will get to it in another step. List *all* of your debts—even loans from Mom and Dad or medical debts that have zero interest. I don't care if there is interest or not. I don't care if some have 24 percent interest and others 4 percent. List the debts smallest to largest! If you were so fabulous with math, you wouldn't have debt, so try this my way. The only time to pay off a larger debt sooner than a smaller one is some kind of big-time emergency such as owing the IRS and having them come after you, or in situations where there will be a foreclosure if you don't pay it off. Otherwise, don't argue about it; just list the debts smallest to largest.

The reason we list smallest to largest is to have some quick wins. This is the "behavior modification over math" part I referred to earlier. Face it, if you go on a diet and lose weight the first week, you will stay on that diet. If you go on a diet and gain weight or go six weeks with no visible progress, you will quit. When training salespeople, I try to get them a sale or two quickly because that fires them up. When you start the debt snowball and in the first few days pay off a couple of little debts, trust me, it lights your fire. I don't care if you have a master's degree in psychology; you need quick wins to get fired up. And getting fired up is super-important.

It's funny to think that at first, I didn't even realize we had a problem. But I started listening to Dave on the radio and read *The Total Money Makeover*, and I got scared. We realized that we were one accident or one job loss away from losing all we had. We simply made too much money to have six-figure debt, not including our home.

It all started after we graduated, loaded with $60,000 in student-loan debt; we did what was normal. We bought a house, two new cars, and took on an additional $35,000 in credit-card debt. We just didn't bother—we weren't trying to keep up with anyone or buy a lot of miscellaneous stuff over time—we just failed to care.

It was the budget that allowed us to communicate in ways we never had before. When we saw that we could clear up a lot of debt in a relatively short period of time instead of the ten to twenty years we originally thought it would take, a huge amount of stress was suddenly lifted off of Amanda.

The thirty-five months working on the debt snowball was the hardest part, but we never wavered. Yes, we had visits from Murphy—having a baby plus Amanda's back surgery and other emergencies, to name a few— but we did it! We actually reached our goal of becoming DEBT-FREE!

We sold our brand-new Jeep Liberty (Amanda really loved that Jeep) and bought a gently used 1991 model. Amanda took on an extra shift at work, and I took over extra tasks around the house to compensate. We scaled back our lifestyle considerably and folks made fun of us, which told us we were on the right track. We knew that we couldn't wander out of debt like we wandered into it.

Our entire paradigm shifted. For the six years we've been married, we've always had debt. We have yet to have a major argument over money since we started this plan. We know that we can do anything we want in a short time. We literally changed our family tree—all because we bothered and cared enough to do something about it.

**Steven (age 32) and
Amanda (age 31) Farrar**
eBay Store Owner; Pharmacist

One lady took her debt snowball form to the local copy shop and had it enlarged to supersize. She then put her huge debt snowball on the refrigerator. Every time she paid off another debt, she drew a big red line through that debt, now gone forever. She told me that every time she walked through the kitchen and looked at that refrigerator door, she would yell, "Oh yeah, we are getting out of debt!" If that sounds corny to you, you are still not getting it. This lady has a PhD. She is not a dumb person. She is so sophisticated and intelligent that she got it. She under-stood that her Total Money Makeover was about a change in behavior, and that behavioral change is best enhanced by some quick (although small) wins.

When you pay off a nagging $52 medical bill or that $122 cell-phone bill from eight months ago, your life is not changed that much mathematically yet. You have, however, begun a process that works, and you have seen it work, and you will keep doing it because you will be fired up about the fact that it works.

After you list the debts smallest to largest, pay the minimum payment to stay current on all the debts except the smallest. Every dollar you can find from anywhere in your budget goes toward the smallest debt until it is paid. Once the smallest is paid, the payment from that debt, plus any extra "found" money, is added to the next smallest debt. (Trust me, once you get going, you will find money.) Then, when debt number two is paid off, you take the money that you used to pay on number one and number two and you pay it, plus any found money, on number three. When three is paid, you attack four, and so on. Keep paying minimums on all the debts except the smallest until it is paid. Every time you pay one off, the amount you pay on the next one down increases. All the money from old debts and all the money you can find anywhere goes on the smallest until it is gone. Attack! Every time the snowball rolls over, it picks up more snow and gets larger, and by the time you get to the bottom, you have an avalanche.

Most people get to the bottom of the list and find that now they can pay well over $1,000 per month on a car loan or a student loan. At that point, it won't take long to bust out and be debt-free except for the house. That is Baby Step Two: Pay Off All Debt (Except the House) Using the Debt Snowball to become debt-free except for your home.

My wife and I were under twenty-five and had over $169,000 in debt. We were sick and tired of being sick and tired! Our debt had grown little by little. Amy would buy small things like clothes and stuff for the house that seemed to nickel and dime us to death. I, on the other hand, would blow money on a larger scale. For example, I bought a BMW (for Amy, of course) and took her on a surprise vacation to New York City. We did not yet have the discipline to tell that inner child to shut up long enough for us to think before we made a purchase.

We did not have the urgency to get rid of our huge amount of debt until a turn in events changed our mindset. Several years ago I changed jobs, which required a training period that decreased my monthly income by $4,000. We had some money in savings, but it quickly dwindled. To start our Total Money Makeover, we decided we had to lower our overhead, sell everything but the kids (maybe), and change our spending habits.

We got crazy and sold our rental property, and we paid off the BMW, department-store card, medical bills, and student loan. We were invited to do fun stuff, and to spend money doing it, but we held off. We decided to have a garage sale that ended up looking like an estate sale; we ate "creative" meals; and then I committed what some people would consider the ultimate sin: I sold my wife's BMW. We knew if our family of four could just make it through these six months living on only $1,700 a month, we could ultimately change our family tree. And we did it! We became debt-free except for the house and were named one of The Total Money Makeover finalists!

The most important part of this whole process was learning to delay pleasure. It's like Dave says: "Live like no one else, so later you can live like no one else!"

Josh (age 26) and
Amy (age 25) Hopkins
Mortgage Loan Officer; Stay-at-Home Mom

The Elements of Making It Work

When I first started teaching this more than thirty years ago, I didn't understand what all the elements of success were or all the clarifications that would be needed. The major elements of making the debt snowball work are using a budget, getting current before you start, smallest-to-largest payoff (no cheating), sacrifice, and focused intensity. Total, sold-out, focused intensity is possibly the most important. This means saying to yourself (and meaning it), *To the exclusion of virtually everything else, I'm getting out of debt!* If you take an old-fashioned magnifying glass outside and set it near some crumpled newspapers, nothing will happen. If you point the sun's rays through the magnifying glass but move it around or wiggle it, nothing will happen. If you hold really still and focus the sun's rays totally on that crumpled newspaper, things begin to happen. Focused intensity will cause you to smell something burning, and soon you will see an actual fire.

If you think this debt snowball stuff is cute and you might sort of give it a try, it won't work. Total, sold-out, focused intensity is required to win. Aiming at the goal and nothing else is the only way to win. You have to know where you are going, and by definition know where you aren't going, or you will never get there. I fly a lot, and I never get on a plane and think to myself, *I wonder where this plane is heading?* I know where I want to go, and if I'm heading to New York, I stay off the plane heading to Detroit. When I get off the plane, I don't catch the first cab I see and say, "Why don't we just drive around awhile because I don't have a plan?" I tell them the hotel and street where I want to go. I then ask how long that will take and what the fare will be. My point is that we don't wander aimlessly around in any other parts of our lives, but we seem to think that will work with money. You can't get ready, fire, and *then* aim with money, and you can't try to do six things at the same time. You are trying to get out of debt. Period. You will have to focus with great intensity to do it.

Proverbs 6:1 and 5 (loosely Dave-paraphrased) says, "If you have signed surety, my son, [*surety* is Bible talk for debt] . . . deliver your-self like the bird from the hand of the fowler and the gazelle from the hand of the hunter." I remember reading that Bible verse in my daily Bible study one day and thinking what a cute little animal metaphor it was for getting out of debt. Then one day later that week I was surfing channels and hit the Discovery Channel. I noticed they were filming gazelles. The gazelles were peacefully gazelling around. Of course, you know the Discovery Channel wasn't there just for the gazelles. The next camera shot was of Mr. Cheetah sneaking up in the bushes looking for lunch in all the right places. Suddenly, one of the gazelles got a whiff of Mr. Cheetah and became very aware of his plan. The other gazelles noticed the alarm and soon also were on edge. They couldn't yet see the cheetah, so out of fear of running at him, they froze until he played his cards.

Realizing he had been discovered, Mr. Cheetah decided to give it his best shot and leaped from the bushes. The gazelles all yelled, "Cheetah!" Well, not really, but they did run like crazy in fourteen different directions. The Discovery Channel that day reminded viewers that the cheetah is the fastest mammal on dry land; he can go from zero to forty-five miles per hour in four leaps. The show also proved that because the gazelle will outmaneuver the cheetah instead of outrunning him, the cheetah will tire quickly. As a matter of fact, the cheetah only gets his gazelle burger for lunch in one out of nineteen chases. The gazelle's primary hunter is the fastest mammal on dry ground, yet the gazelle wins almost every time. Likewise, the way out of debt is to outmaneuver the enemy and *run for your life*.

Around our office, the counselors can predict who will make it out of debt based on how "gazelle-intense" they are. If they are looking at a red line on the refrigerator door and yelling, they have a really good shot. However, if they are looking for a get-rich-quick scheme or some intellectual theory instead of sacrifice, hard work, and total focus, we give them a really low gazelle rating and a low probability of becoming debt-free.

I was first introduced to Dave through his radio show *The Ramsey Show*. I was hooked right away. I was really inspired to read *The Total Money Makeover* and signed myself up to be a facilitator of Dave's *Financial Peace University* at my church. His principles just make sense. They are so simple and very relevant to everyone. I simply needed to wake up and start paying more attention to my spending habits. It was all up to me.

Immediately after beginning his plan and creating a budget, I realized how stupid I had been. I spent too much of my life wasting so much money! With a cash-flow plan in place, I felt more in control. I was telling my money where it should go instead of wondering where it went. It was a very freeing experience.

Once I made the decision to change my mindset and start living more responsibly, I was ready to embrace the seven Baby Steps. My first inclination was to save money first, invest in retirement, and then pay off my debt. I was so wrong. If I had done it my way, I would still be struggling. I would still be enslaved to my lenders.

Starting the debt snowball really got me fired up. It was amazing to see my debt gradually become smaller and smaller while my Snowball became larger and larger. I was so proud of my progress that became more and more evident with every month. Just to be able to make small accomplishments made a tremendous amount of difference. It continuously gave me hope throughout this process. Granted, I did not have or earn a lot of money to put toward becoming debt-free. But I think that made it all the more incredible. I knew I just had to make it work. The ability to become debt-free isn't contingent upon a certain income. It is all about changing behavior and being intense about getting rid of that nasty debt!

Years ago I was simply ignorant when it came to debt. My family didn't talk about that stuff. I just thought debt was something everyone had. Thank God I now know differently and can start living the life I deserve!

DeLisa Dangerfield (age 42)
Registered Nurse

An obvious step to working the debt snowball is to stop borrowing. Otherwise, you will just be changing the names of the creditors on your debt list. So you must draw a line in the sand and say, "I will never borrow again." As soon as you make that statement, there will be a test. Trust me. Your transmission will go out. Your kid will need braces. It is almost as if God wants to see if you are really gazelle-intense. At this point, you are ready for a plastectomy—plastic surgery to cut up your credit cards. I'm often asked, "Dave, should I cut my cards up now or when I pay them off?" Cut them up NOW. A permanent change in your view of debt is your only chance. No matter what happens, you have to pursue the opportunity or solve the challenge without debt. It has to stop. If you think you can get out of debt without huge resolve to stop borrowing, you are wrong. You can't get out of a hole by digging out the bottom.

How to Get the Snowball Rolling

Sometimes your debt snowball won't roll. When some people do their budget, there is barely enough to make all the minimum payments and nothing extra to pay on the smallest. There is no push to get the Snowball rolling. Let me offer another image to help you better understand this problem and the solution. My great-great-grandfather ran a timber operation in the hills of Kentucky and West Virginia. In that bygone era, after cutting the timber, they would put the logs into the river to float them downstream to the sawmill. The logs would build up at a bend in the river, and a traffic jam of wood occurred. This would continue as long as the jammed-up area stopped the progress of the other logs. Sometimes the loggers could break the jam loose by pushing the logs. Other times they would have to get radical before a real mess occurred.

When it got bad, they would break the logjam by throwing dynamite into the middle of the logs that were blocking the progress. As you can imagine, this created a dramatic effect. When the dynamite blew, logs and pieces of logs would fly into the air. After working so hard to cut the trees, some of them were a total loss. They had to blow up some of the timber to get the rest of the crop to market. That's the sacrifice the situation required. Sometimes that is what you have to do with the stopped-up budget. You have to dynamite it. You have to get radical to get the money flowing again.

One way to do that is to sell something. You could sell lots of little stuff at a garage sale, or sell a seldom-used item on the Internet. Get gazelle-intense and sell so much stuff that the kids are afraid they are next. Sell things that make your broke friends question your sanity. If your budget is stopped up and your debt snowball won't roll on its own, you are going to have to get radical.

In watching heroes across the nation get out of debt with gazelle intensity, believe me, I have seen them sell things. One lady sold 350 goldfish from her pond for a dollar apiece. Men have sold their Harleys, boats, knife collections, or baseball cards. Women have sold precious things like nonfamily antiques (keep the heirlooms because you can't get them back) or a personal car they thought was necessary to life on the planet. I don't recommend selling your home unless you have payments above 45 percent of your monthly take-home pay. Usually, the home isn't the problem. I do recommend that most people sell the car with the most debt on it. A good rule of thumb on items (except the house) is this: if you can't be debt-free on it (not counting the home) in eighteen to twenty months, sell it. If you have a car or a boat that you can't pay off in eighteen to twenty months, sell it. It is just a car; dynamite the logjam! I used to love my car, too, but I found keeping that huge debt while trying to get out of debt was like running a race wearing ankle weights. Get a Total Money Makeover, so later you can drive anything you want and pay cash for it. When it comes to that debt-ridden item, you may have to make the decision to live like no one else; but remember, later you will be living, or driving, like no one else.

My wife and I considered credit cards to be just a way of life. It seemed "normal" to simply throw down the cards for everyday items. Vacation rentals, gas, clothes, food—you name it, we paid for it with plastic. Eventually, all of those charges started piling up. It was a gradual and steady accumulation of debt that just kept growing and growing. It was like a snowball that was chasing us instead of us pushing it. All this time I had left my wife to handle the money and didn't give it a second thought, which wasn't fair to her. The next thing we knew, we were $30,000 in debt and in need of a Total Money Makeover.

We had four credit cards with different balances totaling around $25,000. The other $5,000 we owed to the IRS. That was really scary. Needless to say, we attacked the IRS debt first and furiously knocked it out in just three months. Once we were current with all of our payments, we started attacking the credit-card debt. We threw every spare dime we could at it. Today we are debt-free except for the house, and we are building our three-to-six-month emergency fund.

It was definitely hard learning how to say "NO!" to ourselves. For the first time as a couple, we knew we had to make a budget and really stick to it. It wasn't as easy as it sounds, but the payoff has been immeasurable. Once we got used to this lifestyle, everything just seemed to be less stressful. We found contentment and became happier than we had ever been.

I know now that this debt was as much my fault as it was my wife's. Just because we agreed she'd be in charge of the budget didn't let me off the hook. I realize now that it was wrong to leave her to handle all the financial responsibilities. If a spouse has been keeping financial secrets, it's definitely for the best to get them out in the open. It's the only way these problems can get solved. There may be some anger at first and even some feelings of betrayal. Nevertheless, a marriage can only improve with unobstructed communication. The key is to hang on to each other and enjoy the ride out of the mess that you BOTH created.

Jeff (age 41) and
Teresa (age 41) Eller
Owner of a Dump Truck Company;
Medical Manager

The number of people I talk to about this who will not throw dynamite into their logjam to get the money flowing makes me sad. They can see that the logs will never get to market, they will never have wealth, but they just can't stand the thought of blowing up a few of them so the rest will get down the river. Translation: "I love my stupid car more than the idea of becoming wealthy enough to give cars away." Don't make that mistake.

There is another method of breaking your logjam that the lumberjacks didn't have available to them. More water would have pushed the logs around that corner, too, if they could have flooded the river. I may be stretching this metaphor, but more income will also break up your logjam; it will push the Snowball. If your budget is too tight to get the debt snowball rolling, you need to do something to increase income. Selling debt-ridden items lowers the outgo, and selling other items temporarily increases your income. Likewise, working extra hours can increase income in order to increase the speed of debt repayment.

I don't like the idea of working one hundred hours per week, but sometimes extreme situations require extreme solutions. Temporarily, just for a manageable period of time, the extra job or overtime may be your solution. I met Randy while doing a book signing in a major city. Randy was two months from being debt-free. He was twenty-six years old and had paid off $78,000 in debt in twenty-one months. He sold a car and worked ten hours a day, seven days a week. Randy was not a doctor or a lawyer; he was a plumber. Some lawyers would argue that plumbers make more than they do, and in some cases they might be right. Randy's one-man plumbing company had prospered. He had already worked that morning before coming with his wife and little girl to the bookstore. His wife smiled as she looked at her husband with deep respect and told me she hadn't seen him much this last year, but it was going to be worth it soon. Can you imagine the pressure that young marriage must have been under with $78,000 in debt? Now they were almost free.

Randy got radical. He used income to bust the logjam. He promised me he was going to slow down as soon as the debt was paid so he could spend time with his wife and little girl. Now they will be able to go places as a family and do things their debt would never have allowed them to do.

DAVE RANTS . . .

Bad Idea: Separate Checking Accounts

Here's the deal. When you get married, you become a team. The pastor at your wedding wasn't joking when he said, "And now you are one." It's called unity. The old marriage vows say, "Unto thee I pledge all my worldly goods." In other words, "I'm all in," so combine the checking accounts.

It's hard to have unity when you separate your bank accounts. When *his* money is over here, and *her* money is over there, it's easy to live in your own little financial world instead of working as a team.

When you do your spending together, it's about *our* money. *We* have an income and *we* have expenses and *we* have goals. So when you're both in agreement on where the money is going, then you've taken a major step to being on the same page in your marriage, and you will create awesome levels of communication.

This all boils down to trust. Do you trust your spouse or not? I've heard from people who keep separate bank accounts *just in case* their spouse leaves them. Well, why on earth would you marry someone you can't trust? And if that's really the case, then you need marriage counseling, not separate bank accounts!

Your spouse isn't your roommate, and this isn't a joint business venture. It's a marriage! You don't run your household and your life separately. Your job is to love each other well, and that includes having shared financial goals—which is hard to do when you have separate accounts.

I picked up a pizza one night, and as the guy behind the counter started walking toward his car with a stack of pizzas to be delivered, he saw me and stopped. Smiling, he said, "Hey, Dave, I'm here because of you. Only three more months, and I'm debt-free!" This was not some seventeen-year-old teenager; this was a dad, a thirty-five-year-old guy who wanted to be free.

There is a young single guy who works on my team. He is gazelle-intense about becoming debt-free. He works here until 5:30 every day, and he smiles as he leaves to work for UPS for another four or five hours virtually every night.

Why are these guys all smiling? They work hard and unbelievable extra hours, so why would they smile? They smile because they have caught the vision, the vision of living like no one else so later they can live like no one else.

What About Saving for Retirement While the Snowball's Rolling?

Matt asked me on the radio show about another subject people have trouble with on Baby Step Two. Matt wanted to know if he should stop his 401(k) contributions to get his debt snowball moving. He really didn't want to stop contributing, especially the first 3 percent because his company matches that 100 percent. I am a math nerd, and I know the 100 percent match is sweet, but I have seen something more powerful—focused intensity. If you are going to be gazelle-intense and do everything in your power to become debt-free very quickly, then stop your retirement plan contributions, even if your company matches them. The power of focus and quick wins is more important in the long term to your Total Money Makeover than is the match. This is only for people who have already pulled out all the stops and are ready for "anything goes" to become debt-free quickly.

If you are radically gazelle-intense, the speed of your debt freedom will enable you to return to that 401(k) with the match in just a matter of months. Imagine how much you'll be able to contribute without payments. The average person who throws the dynamite and is gazelle-intense will be debt-free except for his or her home in eighteen months. Some take longer and others less, depending on debt, income, and savings at the time they start their Total Money Makeover. If for some reason you are stuck in an extremely deep hole, you may want to continue doing some retirement saving. An extremely deep hole is NOT defined by your unwillingness to apply yourself.

An extremely deep hole is not Phil's situation. Phil makes $120,000 per year and has $70,000 of debt, $32,000 of which is on one car. Sell the car and amputate the lifestyle, Phil. Phil should be debt-free in nine months, no excuses and no prisoners. An extremely deep hole is Tammy's situation. Tammy has $74,000 in student loans with another $15,000 in credit-card debt. Tammy is a single mom with three children and has an income of $50,000 per year. It is going to take Tammy a few years to work her debt snowball. She will figure a way through it, but her situation is one of the very rare exceptions; she should keep contributing to the 401(k) with the match.

When You Have to Dip into the Emergency Fund

Penny's air conditioner went out in the dead of summer. The repairs were $650, which she took from her emergency fund. "Thank goodness that $1,000 was there," she said with a sigh. Now what does she do? The debt snowball, or stop and go back to Baby Step One (save $1,000)? Penny needs to put the debt snowball temporarily on hold. She will continue to make minimum payments and go back to the first step until she gets back up to $1,000 in her emergency fund. If she doesn't, soon she will have nothing in savings, and when the alternator on the car goes out, she will reopen some credit-card account. The same applies to you. If you use the emergency fund, return to Baby Step One until you have re-funded your beginner emergency fund; then move right back to your debt snowball, Baby Step Two.

Second Mortgages, Business Debt, and Rental Property Mortgages

Because of debt-consolidation loans and other mistakes, many people have a home equity loan or some kind of large second mortgage. What should be done with this loan? Is it put in the debt snowball, or just called a mortgage and not dealt with at this step? It will be paid off; it is just a matter of at which step. Generally speaking, if your second mortgage is more than 50 percent of your gross annual income, you should not put it in the debt snowball. We will get to it later. If you make $40,000 per year and have a $15,000 second mortgage, you should put it in the debt snowball. Let's just take care of it now. But if you have a $35,000 second mortgage and make $40,000, you will get to it in another step. By the way, you should consider refinancing your first and second mortgages together if you can lower both interest rates. Then put the total on a fifteen-year mortgage, or the remaining years of your current first mortgage, whichever is less (e.g., if you have twelve years remaining on your first mortgage at 9 percent interest, refinance the first and second mortgages together into a new first at 6 percent over twelve years or less).

Many small-business owners have debt and want to know how to handle that debt in the debt snowball. Most small-business debt is personally guaranteed, which means it is really personal debt. If you have a small-business loan of $15,000 at the bank or have borrowed on your credit cards for business, this is personal debt. Treat small-business debt like any other kind of debt. List it with all your other debts, smallest to largest, in the debt snowball. If your business debt is larger than half your gross annual income or half your home mortgage, hold the payoff on that size debt until later. Smaller and medium-sized debts are what we want to pay off at this step.

The only other larger debts to delay are mortgages on rental properties. Stop buying more rental property, but hold that debt until later. After your home mortgage is paid off in a later Baby Step, you should snowball your rental mortgages. List the rental debts smallest to largest, and concentrate all your focus on the smallest until paid. Then work your way through the rest. If you own several, or even just one, rental property, you should consider selling some or all to get the money to pay off the ones you keep or pay off other debt listed in the debt snowball. Having $40,000 in credit-card debt and a rental with $40,000 equity doesn't make sense. You wouldn't borrow $40,000 on credit cards to buy a rental, I hope. So why would you keep the situation described here, which has the same effect?

Other than the home mortgage, larger second mortgages, business loans, and rental mortgages are the only things that aren't paid off in Baby Step Two (Pay Off All Debt (Except the House) Using the Debt Snowball). With gazelle intensity, great focus, extreme sacrifice, selling things, and working extra, we clear all debt. Again, if you are fired up, normally this will happen within eighteen to twenty months. Some will get out of debt sooner, and some will get out in a slightly longer period of time. If your Snowball is scheduled to run longer, never fear; it may not take as long as the math seems to indicate. Many people find a way to shorten the time with sheer intensity, and God tends to pour blessings on people going in a direction He wants them to go. It is as if you are walking or running at a fast pace, and a moving sidewalk suddenly appears below you to carry you faster than your own effort would.

The debt snowball is very possibly the most important step in your Total Money Makeover for two reasons. One, you free up your most powerful wealth-building tool, your income, during this step. Two, you take on the entire American culture by declaring war on debt. By paying off your debt, you make a statement about your stance on the issue of debt. By paying off your debt, you show that The Total Money Makeover of your heart has occurred, paving the way for a Total Money Makeover of your actual wealth.

Scan this QR code to sign up for EveryDollar and start budgeting for free.

8

Finish the Emergency Fund: Kick Murphy Out

Close your eyes and think about what it will be like when you reach this Baby Step. Most gazelle-intense participants in a Total Money Makeover will arrive at the beginning of Baby Step Three (Save Three to Six Months of Expenses in a Fully Funded Emergency Fund) in around eighteen to twenty months. When you reach this step, you have $1,000 cash and no debt except your home mortgage. You have pushed with such focused intensity that the ball is now rolling, and you have momentum on your side. Again, close your eyes and breathe in. Think about what it will feel like when you are debt-free except for the house and have $1,000 cash. Did I see you smiling?

You are beginning to see the power of being in control of your largest wealth-building tool, your income. Now that you don't have any payments except the house, Baby Step Three should come quickly.

Baby Step Three: Save Three to Six Months of Expenses in a Fully Funded Emergency Fund

A fully funded emergency fund covers three to six months of expenses.

What would it take for you to live three to six months if you lost your income? Financial planners and financial counselors like myself have used this rule of thumb for years, and it has served my Total Money Makeover participants well. You start the emergency fund with $1,000, but a fully funded emergency fund will usually range from $10,000 to $25,000. The typical family that can make it on $3,000 per month might have a $10,000 emergency fund as a minimum. What would it feel like to have no payments but the house, and $10,000 in savings for when it rains?

Remember what we said about emergencies a couple of chapters back? It *will* rain; you need an umbrella. Don't forget, *Money* magazine says that 78 percent of us will have a major unexpected event within the next ten years. When the big stuff happens, like the job layoff or the blown car engine, you can't depend on credit cards. If you use debt to cover emergencies, you have backtracked again. A well-designed Total Money Makeover will walk you out of debt forever. A strong foundation in your financial house includes the big savings account, which will be used just for emergencies.

After my divorce, I found myself homeless, pregnant, and raising my eighteen-month-old son alone. Plus, I was stuck with all the debt from the failed marriage! I went from two incomes and one child, to one income and two children. I started living off of credit cards out of necessity, racking up piles of debt as I went along. I moved into public housing and lived there for two years, trying to take care of my kids and stay current on the bills.

It was tough feeling like I couldn't provide for my family; I wanted more for my children. They have gone without birthday parties and other little things that kids their age have. They have never had a place to call home, and that's my strongest drive in getting out of debt.

I know firsthand the importance of an emergency fund. For the first time in my life, I had money in the bank when my truck broke down. I didn't have to go into debt, and my income wasn't affected. I just paid the mechanic and refilled my emergency fund as soon as possible. Then I went right back to paying off my debts. It was time-consuming and tedious, but worth it to have the security that the emergency fund provided.

It hasn't been easy. Just about every time I've gotten within a few dollars of having my emergency fund back in place, something has happened, and I've had to use it again. But it is now standard practice to refill my emergency fund whenever I use it—it has saved my family from a lot of hard times and from going further into debt.

Rebecca Gonzalez (age 28)
Human Resources Assistant

I'm going to bang on this drum again because it is vital if your makeover is going to be permanent. The worst time to borrow is when times are bad. If there is a recession and you lose your job (read, "no income"), you don't want to have a bunch of debt. In a recent study by the Federal Reserve, 36 percent of Americans said they would borrow on a credit card if a rainy day came, and it wouldn't be difficult. I agree it wouldn't be difficult because credit cards are issued to dogs and dead people every year, but that doesn't mean it would be smart. What would be difficult is to make the payments and even pay off the debt if you don't get that new replacement job. Our own research says 48 percent of Americans do not have an emergency fund that could cover three months of expenses. One-third have no savings at all. Half of this culture has virtually no buffer between them and life. Here comes Murphy! Remember how we discussed that problems seem to be (and I believe actually are) less frequent when you have your fully funded emergency fund? Don't forget that the emergency fund actually acts as Murphy repellent.

So, what is an emergency, anyway? An emergency is something you had no way of knowing was coming, something that has a major impact on you and your family if you don't cover it. Emergencies include paying the deductible on medical, homeowner's, or car insurance after an accident; a job loss or cutback; medical bills resulting from an accident or unforeseen medical problem; or a blown transmission or engine in a car that you need to function. All of these are emergencies. Something on sale that you "need" is not an emergency. Fixing the boat, unless you live on it, is not an emergency. "I want to start a business" is not an emergency. "I want to buy a car or a leather couch or go to Cancún" is not an emergency. Prom dresses and college tuition are not emergencies. Beware not to rationalize the use of your emergency fund for something that you should save for and purchase. On the other hand, don't make payments on medical bills after an accident while your emergency fund sits there fully funded. If you've gone to the trouble of creating an emergency fund, make sure you are crystal clear on what is and is not an emergency.

Before using the emergency fund, back up from the situation and calm down. Sharon and I would never use the emergency fund without first discussing it and being in agreement. We also would never use the emergency fund without sleeping on the decision and praying about it. Our agreement, our prayer, and our cooling-off period all help us determine if this decision is a rationalization, a reaction, or a real emergency.

The Emergency Fund Must Be Easy to Access

Keep your emergency fund in something that is liquid. *Liquid* is a money term that means easy to get to with no penalties. If you would hesitate to use the fund because of the penalties you'll incur to get to it, you have it in the wrong place. I use growth-stock mutual funds for long-term investing, but I would never put my emergency fund there. If my car engine blew, I would be tempted to borrow to fix it rather than cash in my mutual fund because the market is down (we always want to wait on it to go back up). That means I have the emergency fund in the wrong place. Mutual funds are good long-term investments, but because of market fluctuations, you are likely to have an emergency when the market is down—another invitation to Murphy. So keep your emergency fund liquid!

For the same reason, don't use certificates of deposit for your emergency fund because typically you will be charged a penalty for making an early withdrawal. The exception to this is if you can get some kind of "quick-release" CD that allows one withdrawal during the committed period without penalty. That quick release makes the money available to you without penalty and would make that CD a good emergency fund. Understand, you don't want to "invest" the emergency fund, just have it someplace safe and easy to get to.

If you already have emergency-fund money someplace it shouldn't be, use your head if a true emergency hits you. Christine, a sixty-nine-year-old grandmother, told me she borrowed to fix her transmission because she didn't want to pay a penalty to cash out her CD. The loan was her "wise" banker's suggestion, and Christine trusted her banker. The only problem is, even with the penalty, Christine would have been better off to cash out her CD. The repair cost was $3,000. Her CD earned 5 percent, and the penalty for cashing it out early was half the interest. So her banker loaned her $3,000 at 9 percent interest so she wouldn't lose 2.5 percent in penalties. Doesn't sound too wise to me. Honestly, it doesn't sound too ethical to me either. Words are powerful; none of us want to be "penalized." When emotions took over, Christine trusted instead of thinking and made a bad decision.

I suggest a money market account with no penalties and a debit card or check-writing privileges for your emergency fund. We have a large emergency fund for our household in a mutual-fund company money market account. Wherever you get your mutual funds, look at the website to find money market accounts that pay interest equal to one-year CDs. I haven't found bank money market accounts to be competitive. The FDIC does not insure the mutual-fund money market accounts, but I keep mine there anyway because I've never known one to fail. Keep in mind that the interest earned is not the main thing. The main thing is that the money is available to cover emergencies. Your wealth building is not going to happen in this account; that will come later, in other places. This account is more like insurance against rainy days than it is investing.

Sometimes, even after I've explained all this, people still ask about savings bonds, bonds, or other "low-risk" investments. They are missing the point. Again, this emergency fund is not for wealth building. You will get other kinds of return on investment from this account, but the purpose of this money is not to make you rich. The mission statement for the emergency fund is to protect you against storms, give you peace of mind, and keep the next problem from becoming debt.

How Big?

So, how much money should be in your emergency fund? We said it should be enough to cover three to six months of expenses, but should you go with three months or six months? If you think about the purpose of this fund, it will help you determine what is right for you. The purpose of the fund is to absorb risk, so the more risky your situation, the greater the emergency fund you should have. For example, if you earn straight commission or are self-employed, you should use the six-months rule. If you are single or you are a one-income married household, you should use the six-months rule because a job loss in your situation is a 100 percent cut in household income. If your job situation is unstable or there are chronic medical problems in the family, you, too, should lean toward the six-months rule.

I grew up in government-assisted housing (the projects) and, for a long time, thought that's how the remainder of my life was supposed to be lived. However, when I was twenty-four years old, the Lord provided me with a job that challenged me intellectually and continually pushed me to think outside the box. I began to listen to the news and political discussions on the radio, and one day I happened to stumble across a funny white guy named Dave.

After listening to Dave, it took a few years for my wife and me to get onboard. When we finally did decide to have a Total Money Makeover, the hardest part was getting mad enough to eliminate all our debt at once. We continued to make purchases on our credit card and would find ourselves back at square one. But reality set in once I was laid off from my job. We couldn't afford to make ends meet. I felt like such a failure because I knew that if I had stuck to Dave's plan and advice, we would have been in a much better situation.

After that initial layoff, we struggled for a while until I finally landed a new job. Yet we have become debt-free because we work together and do our part to assure the financial success of our present and future. The level of accountability that is required is tremendous! We fought a lot at the beginning, but as we've worked through things, our communication has become smooth and hassle-free. We have been patient and diligent in our budgeting and are now reaping the benefits!

Our family is still realizing the full impact of being debt-free. The month after we paid off the debt, I was laid off again. But this time we were in a completely different place than before. The financial worries and strains were nonexistent. There is a sense of peace that surpasses all understanding, and until you have experienced it for yourself, you can't even imagine its amazing power.

**James (age 32) and
Tabitha (age 31) Atwood**
*Train Conductor; Merchandising
Coordinator*

If you have a "steady, secure" job where you have been with that company or government agency for fifteen years and everyone is healthy, you could lean toward the three-month rule. A real estate agent should have a six-month fund, and a healthy, tenured teacher who plans to stay at her job long term might keep a three-month fund. Customize your emergency fund to your situation and to how your spouse deals with the feeling of risk. Many times men and women deal with this subject differently. This fund is for actual protection and for peace of mind, so the spouse who wants this fund to be higher wins.

We use three to six months of expenses instead of three to six months of income because the fund is to cover expenses, not replace income. If you become ill or lose a job, you need to keep the lights on and food on the table until things turn around, but you might stop investing, and you'll definitely stop spending budgeted "blow money" until the rain clears. Of course, when you are just starting your Total Money Makeover, your expenses might equal your income. Later, when you are debt-free, you have all the right insurance in place, and you have large investments, you can survive on much less than your income.

Use All Available Cash

In Baby Step Two, I instructed you to use all nonretirement savings and investments to pay down your debt. Clean everything out and become debt-free except for the house. Use all savings and investments that don't have a penalty for withdrawal, like retirement plans. If you used savings that you had in Baby Step Two (Pay Off All Debt (Except the House) Using the Debt Snowball), you cleaned out even the emergency fund down to Baby Step One (Save $1,000 for Your Starter Emergency Fund). Now is the time to rebuild your emergency fund by replacing any money you may have used to pay debt. Many times I've met someone who, for example, had $6,000 in savings at the bank making 2 percent interest, and $11,000 in credit-card debt. The very thought of using $5,000 of that savings to pay the credit cards partially off is very hard. That $6,000 emergency fund is your security blanket, and fear rises up deep inside when someone like me mentions that you should use that money to snowball your debt. You are right to feel that fear and to question whether you should spend the $5,000 to pay down the debt. You should use that money ONLY if you and your whole family are into a Total Money Makeover. Gazelle intensity, budgeting, selling ankle-weight cars, and overall total commitment to the plan are the only ways using that savings makes sense.

You Need All Parties Completely Onboard

Sherry called our radio show saying that her husband wanted to use $9,000 of their $10,000 emergency fund on Baby Step Two, but he wanted to keep his $21,000 truck debt—with a household income of $43,000. Sherry was mad at me for suggesting something so absurd. Of course, I didn't make that suggestion. I think it would be a bad move for them to use $9,000 in this situation. The reason I'm against using the savings as suggested is that hubby isn't onboard. He wants to do part of the plan and keep his stupid truck. There are two reasons not to use the emergency fund in Sherry's case. First, hubby has not had a Total Money Makeover in his heart, and they will never make it out of debt under any strategy until he does. Second, do the math: on a $43,000 income, they will be in debt and have only a super-small emergency fund for years if they keep the truck. This would be like my wife saying she wants me to lose weight and then baking homemade chocolate-chip cookies every night. She would be saying one thing and doing another.

I don't suggest you clean out your savings if everyone isn't having a Total Money Makeover. I also don't suggest you clean out your savings if you are planning to be in Baby Step Two (Pay Off All Debt (Except the House) Using the Debt Snowball) for five years. However, few of you will be in Step Two very long if you go gazelle-intense and follow this plan to the letter. If your family is exposed to the elements, with only $1,000 standing between you and life for eighteen to twenty months, that is fine. In that case, you should use your savings to become debt-free or accelerate the Snowball.

I know that even if everyone is onboard, gazelle-intense, and there is a plan, my suggestion still scares some of you. Good. Don't you think one of the things that make the gazelle intense is fear? For a short period of time, while you work your debt snowball and rebuild your emergency fund in Step Three, use that fear as a motivator to stay focused and keep everyone else moving.

The good news in Sherry's story is that her hubby heard her on the radio with me, and a lightbulb came on. He sold "his" truck, she used "her" savings, and in fourteen months they were debt-free; in eighteen months

> ## DAVE RANTS . . .
>
> The reason you are afraid of investing is because you do not know what you are getting into. Learn about investments.

they were debt-free with a fully funded emergency fund. Sherry sent an email to me about an amusing part of their journey. She said after they were debt-free and rebuilding her precious emergency fund with the same gazelle intensity they used to pay the debt, one of their teens asked them to buy a computer. Before Sherry could say no, her hubby grabbed the teen in a loving headlock and started yelling, in jest, that there would be no purchases in that house until the emergency fund was done. This made Sherry smile because it told her that not only was the emergency fund coming back soon, but that her husband had gotten the message of how important that fund was to her. She was willing to have a Total Money Makeover, but only if it was Total—for both of them.

Gender and Emergencies

The sexes do view the emergency fund differently. In general, men are more task-oriented, and women are more security-based. Men like to know what you "do," so some of us don't understand the idea of money just sitting there causing security. Most women I meet smile when we start talking about having $10,000 between them and the rain. Many of them say the emergency fund and life insurance are the best parts of their family's Total Money Makeover.

Guys, let's talk. God wired women better on this subject than He did us. Their nature causes them to gravitate toward the emergency fund. Somewhere down inside the typical lady is a "security gland," and when financial stress enters the scene, that gland will spasm. This spasmodic gland will affect your wife in ways you can't always predict. A spasmodic security gland can affect her emotions, her concentration, and even her love life. Apparently, the security gland is attached to her face. Can you see the financial stress on her face? Believe me, guys, one of the best investments you will ever make is in an emergency fund. A fully funded emergency fund and a husband in the midst of a Total Money Makeover will relax the security gland and make your life much better. My friend Jeff Allen, a comedian, does a whole routine on "Happy Wife, Happy Life." The bottom line is that even if you don't "get" the emergency fund, get one.

I already told you that Sharon and I lost everything, went broke, crashed, and were at the bottom, so you can imagine that this subject is a little sensitive at my house. Our financial crash was totally my doing: it was my real estate business screwup that Sharon watched before she took the ride with me. One of the wounds in our relationship is this issue of security. Her emotions can revisit the fear of looking at a brand-new baby and a toddler and not knowing how we were going to keep the heat on. That is a sensitive place in her psyche, and with good reason. We don't even use the emergency fund for emergencies. Part of the salve on that wound is that our emergency fund has an emergency fund. If I even walk near the drawer where the emergency fund money market checkbook is kept, Sharon's security gland can tighten up.

Being the highly trained investment mogul that I am, I could certainly find places to put that money where it would earn more. Or would it? Remember, personal finance is personal. I have come to realize that Sharon's peace of mind bought with the oversized emergency fund is a great return on investment. Guys, this can be a wonderful gift to your wife.

An Emergency Fund Can Turn Crises into Inconveniences

As you budget over the years and your Total Money Makeover completely changes your money habits, you will use the emergency fund less and less. We haven't touched our emergency fund in over twenty years. When we first started, everything was an emergency. But as you crawl off the bottom, and the Total Money Makeover begins to take effect, you have fewer things you can't cover in your monthly budget. At the start, though, you'll be like we were—everything will be an emergency. To show you what I mean, consider two different stories of people at two different places in the Baby Steps.

Kim was twenty-three, single, on her own, and at a job making $27,000 per year. She had recently started her Total Money Makeover. She was behind on credit cards, not on a budget, and barely making her rent because her spending was out of control. She let her car insurance drop because she "couldn't afford it." She did her first budget and two days later was in a car wreck. Since it wasn't bad, the damage to the other guy's car was only about $550. As Kim looked at me through panicked tears, that $550 might as well have been $55,000. She hadn't even started Baby Step One. She was trying to get current, and now she had one more hurdle to clear before she even started. This was a huge emergency.

Seven years ago George and Sally were in the same place. They were broke with new babies, and George's career was sputtering. George and Sally fought and scraped through a Total Money Makeover. Today they are debt-free, even their home. They have a $12,000 emergency fund, retirement in Roth IRAs, and even the kids' college is funded. George has grown personally, his career has blossomed, and he now makes $75,000 per year while Sally stays home with the kids. One day a piece of trash flew out of the back of George's pickup and hit a car behind him on the interstate. The damage was about $550.

I think you can see that George and Sally probably adjusted one month's budget and paid the repairs, while Kim dealt with her wreck for months. The point is that as you get in better shape, it takes a lot more to rock your world. When the accidents occurred, George's heart rate didn't even change, but Kim needed a Valium sandwich to calm down.

Those true stories illustrate the fact that as you progress through your Total Money Makeover, the definition of an emergency that is worthy to be covered by the emergency fund changes. As you have better health insurance, disability insurance, more room in your budget, and better cars, you will have fewer things that qualify as emergency-fund emergencies.

What used to be a huge, life-altering event will become a mere inconvenience. When you are debt-free and aggressively investing to become wealthy, taking a few months off from investing will put a new engine in a car. When I say the emergency fund is Murphy repellent, that is only partially correct. The reality is that Murphy doesn't visit as much, but when he does, we hardly notice his presence. When Sharon and I were broke, our heating-and-air system quit, and the repair cost $580. It was a huge, hairy deal. Recently I had a new $1,300 water heater installed because the old one started leaking, and I hardly noticed. I wonder if the stress relief that your Total Money Makeover provides will allow you to live longer?

Let Me Be Perfectly Clear

There are some Baby Step Three clarifications. Joe asked recently if he should stop his Snowball—Step Two—to get his emergency fund finished. Joe and his wife have twins due in six months. Brad's plant is closing in four months, and he will lose his job. Mike got a huge severance check of $25,000 last week when his company downsized him. Should these people work on debt or finish the emergency fund? All three should temporarily stop snowballing and concentrate on the emergency fund because we can see distant storm clouds that are real. Once the storm passes, they can resume the plan as before.

Resuming the plan for Joe means that once the babies are born healthy, are home, and everyone is fine, Joe will take the emergency fund back down to $1,000 by using the rest of the savings to pay the debt snowball.

Resuming for Brad would mean that once he finds his new job, he'll do the same. Mike should hold his instant emergency fund of $25,000 until he is reemployed. The sooner he can get a job, the more that severance is going to look like a bonus and have a huge impact on the debt snowball.

Sometimes people think they don't need an emergency fund because their income is guaranteed. Richard was retired from the military and received about $4,500 per month, which he could live on if he lost his job. He didn't think he needed an emergency fund because he thought all emergencies were job-related. Then he had a car wreck the same month he was laid off. His $4,500 kept coming, but now he faced car debt. Even if your income is guaranteed, you still might need to help a sick relative, replace your heating system in the middle of winter, or get a new transmission. Large, out-of-budget emergencies that aren't job-related do come up and will require the emergency fund.

If You Don't Own a Home

I keep saying that you are debt-free except for the house at this point and saving to finish the emergency fund. What if you don't have a home yet? When do you save for the down payment? I am going to talk as many of you as possible into the 100 percent down plan, but I know some of you will take the fifteen-year fixed-rate mortgage that I said earlier is okay.

I love real estate, but do not buy a home until you finish this step. A home is a blessing, but if you move into home ownership with debt and no emergency fund, Murphy will set up residence in the spare bedroom. I believe in the financial and emotional advantages of home ownership, but I have known many stressed-out young couples who rushed to buy something before they were ready.

Saving for a down payment or cash purchase of a home should occur after becoming debt-free in Step Two and after finishing the emergency fund in Step Three. That makes saving for a down payment Baby Step Three (b). You should save for the home if you have the itch before moving on to the next step. Many people are worried about getting a home, but please let it be a blessing rather than a curse. It will be a curse if you buy something while you are still broke. There are all sorts of folks who are eager to "work with you" so you can make it happen sooner, but the definition of "creative financing" is "too broke to buy a house."

Next Stop: Serious Wealth Building

Well, you have made it. You are now debt-free except for the home mortgage, and you have three to six months of expenses saved. Getting to the end of this step if you are gazelle-intense takes the typical family twenty-four to thirty months. Two or two and a half years from the time you start your Total Money Makeover, you can sit at the kitchen table with no payments, other than for the house, and with around $10,000 in a money market account. Close your eyes one more time and let your emotions and your spirit visit that place. Wow, I know I see you smiling now.

I'm a single mom of two kids, I own my own company, and I have everything paid off but the house! But it didn't start out that way.

When I was twenty, I became pregnant with my first child and thought my life was over. I had completed two years of college, but I didn't know how I was going to finish my degree and raise a baby, so I left school. Then the next year, I went through a horrible divorce. I didn't know what I was going to do!

I was living off of $400 a month and using credit cards for everything. I went back to school and worked like crazy to graduate a year and a half later. Even though I had a degree in advertising, I couldn't find a job I was excited about. So I decided to start my own cleaning business at age twenty-three.

Word spread and my business grew. At my lowest, I was $100,000 in debt. Over the past six years, though, I've steadily worked my way into becoming debt-free! I worked long, hard hours in order to pay off all the debt that I owed, but it was completely worth it!

Now I have no car payments and have $2 million in term life insurance and disability insurance. I am happy, I'm debt-free, my kids go to a private school, and my retirement plan is set up. Each month, I put away $3,000 for my children's education, the emergency fund, and investments. My house is currently on the market because I want to rent and save up for a huge down payment on my next home. My goal is to be completely debt-free, including the house, by age thirty-five!

Autumn Key (age 29)
Owner of Southern Comfort Cleaning

I am very demanding and very passionate about following these principles and steps precisely because I have seen people (like the ones throughout this book) win doing the Total Money Makeover. I have heard every excuse, every whining reason, and every rationalization as to why you are different and you have a better way, but trust me: you don't.

Once we have covered these basic steps and laid a foundation, the time has come to build some wealth. Remember, that is why we started a Total Money Makeover. We wanted not just to be out of debt, but to become wealthy enough to give, retire with dignity, leave an inheritance, and have some expensive fun. Stay tuned for some big fun.

Your budget is your plan for saving your emergency fund. Scan the QR code below to learn how to prioritize your savings in your budget.

9

Maximize Retirement Investing: Be Financially Healthy for Life

I have a friend in his forties who has a bodybuilder physique. He is lean with well-defined muscle groups, but he is not some wild health nut. He watches what he eats and works out a couple of times a week. I have another friend in his thirties who diets fanatically, runs every day, lifts weights three times a week, but is still forty pounds overweight. The second guy started his health journey a couple of years ago and is losing weight and getting in shape. The first muscleman maintains what he worked hard years ago to get, but he isn't working nearly as hard today.

The Total Money Makeover is the same way. Gazelle intensity is required to get to the wealth steps, but simple maintenance will keep your money muscles maintained. Keep in mind that my muscleman friend never eats three plates of food at a sitting. He is still aware he can lose his fitness, but he can look good and feel good with a lot less effort, assuming he remembers the principles that got him his great body in the first place.

Gazelle intensity has allowed you to lose one hundred pounds of debt and get your cardio emergency fund ready. That foundation will allow you to become financially fit by toning your muscles. You have attacked your debt; it is gone. With the extra money after eliminating your debt, you attacked your emergency fund; it is funded. You are now at a crucial time. What do you do with the extra money that you poured into the emergency fund and debt payoffs? This is not the time to give yourself a raise! You have a plan, and you are winning. Keep it up! You are two quarters into a four-quarter game. It is time to begin with the end in mind! It is time to invest.

What Retirement *Isn't*

Investing for retirement in the context of a Total Money Makeover doesn't necessarily mean investing to quit your job. If you hate your career path, change it. You should do something with your life that lights your fire and lets you use your gifts. Retirement in America has come to mean "save enough money so I can quit the job I hate." That is a bad life plan.

Harold Fisher was one hundred years old. He worked five days a week at the architectural firm he founded. Mr. Fisher didn't work because he needed money, not by a long shot. He worked because he found joy in what he did. He was a designer of churches. His favorite saying was, "People who retire early, die early." "If I retired, what would I do?" he asked. Harold Fisher was financially secure and able to do what he wanted, and that defines *retirement* the Total Money Makeover way.

When I speak of retirement, I think of security. Security means choices. (That's why I think retirement means that work is an option.) You can choose to write a book, to design churches, or to spend time with your grandkids. You need to reach the point where your money works harder than you do. A Total Money Makeover retirement plan means investing with the goal of security. You already possess the ability to quit your job, and if you don't like your work, you should consider doing that. If not today, develop a five-year game plan for transitioning into what God designed you to do; however, don't wait till you're sixty-five to do what you love.

That said, the money part does matter. You want to reach your golden years with financial dignity. That will happen only with a plan. According to a study by the Employee Benefit Research Institute (ERBI), only 18 percent of American workers say they are very confident that they will have enough money when they retire, and half of workers have never even tried to calculate how much money they need to save in order to retire with dignity. Not only have we not done anything about retiring with dignity, we have lost hope that it is even possible. In our *National Study of Millionaires*, we found that most non-millionaires believe you have to come from a wealthy family, get a big inheritance, have a six-figure salary, or just be lucky to have a million dollars for retirement. Wow! These people need a Total Money Makeover in a big way! If you want another peek at the warped view of reality we have, consider that the ERBI also found that 83 percent of retirees are confident that they'll have enough money to take care of basic expenses during retirement. That sounds all well and good, but also consider that the average retiree aged sixty-five and older has only $280,000 saved. That's only going to give them a little over $20,000 annually to live on during their golden years. And with life being as expensive as it is these days (and more expensive as you get older), those "confident" retirees are clearly living in a fantasy!

I grew up poor, so I know the value of a dollar. My grandma raised me, and I watched her struggle every day to provide for us. She taught me early on how important it was to save for a rainy day.

My first job was picking cotton. Eventually I got a job working for a natural gas pipeline, and I worked for that company for thirty-five years. I never made more than $60,000 in any given year, but I always put 10 percent of my check into a stock purchase plan, which is what we used to have instead of a 401(k). At first, I didn't think I could afford to put that much of my paycheck into a retirement plan, but then I figured that, in the long run, I couldn't afford not to.

After thirty-five years on the job, I was able to retire at age fifty-eight—seven years early—with about $1,000,000 in my retirement accounts!

Since retiring, I built myself a workshop and spend a lot of time tinkering in it, just having fun. My wife and I even took a month-long vacation out west—just because it's something we've always wanted to do, and we had the money to do it!

Since we were focused on putting a little money away every month instead of keeping up with the Joneses, we're now free to do whatever we want for the rest of our lives!

**Jim (age 64) and
Kay (age 60) Robinson**
*Both Retired: Former Technical
Specialist; Former Nurse and Stay-at-
Home Mom*

The reality is much colder. Our research says one in three people over the age of sixty doesn't even have $1,000 in savings. Forty-five percent of people sixty and older have household incomes below what is needed to afford basic living needs in their area. And the Social Science Research Network (SSRN) found that there are five times more people sixty-five and older in the U.S. bankruptcy system over the last twenty years. Getting older is going to happen! You must invest now if you want to spend your golden years in dignity. Investing with the long-term goal of security is not a theory to ponder every few years; it is a necessity you must act on now. You must actually fill out the paperwork for your 401(k). You must actually choose your mutual funds and put money in that thing. According to these statistics, the level of denial the average person has on this subject is alarming.

Baby Step Four: Invest 15 Percent of Your Income in Retirement

Those of you concerned about retirement are relieved we have finally gotten to this step. Those who have been living in denial are wondering what all the fuss is about. Baby Step Four is time to get really serious about your wealth building. Remember, when you reach this step you don't have any payments but a house payment, and you have three to six months' worth of expenses in savings, which is thousands of dollars. With only one payment, it should be easy to invest heavily. Even with a below-average income, you can ensure your golden years will have dignity. Before this step, you have ceased or have never started investing, and now you have to really pour on the coals.

Gazelle intensity in the previous steps has allowed you to be able to focus on growing a sizable nest egg. The tens of thousands of people we have met have helped me develop the 15 percent rule. The rule is simple: invest 15 percent of before-tax gross income annually toward retirement. Why not more? You need some of your income left to do the next two steps: college saving and paying off your home early. Why not less? Some people want to invest less or none so they can get a child through school or pay off the home superfast. I don't recommend that because those kids' college degrees won't feed you at retirement. I don't recommend paying off the house first because I have counseled too many seventy-five-year-olds with a paid-for house and no money. They end up selling the family home or mortgaging it to eat. Bad plan. You need some retirement investing at this stage before saving for college and the mortgage payoff. Plus, by getting started now, the magic of compound growth will work for you.

When calculating your 15 percent, don't include company matches in your plan. Invest 15 percent of your gross income. If your company matches some or part of your contribution, you can consider it gravy. Remember, this is a rule of thumb, so if you cheat down to 12 percent or up to 17 percent, that is not a huge problem, but understand the dangers of straying far from 15 percent. If you underinvest, you will one day be buying that classic cookbook *72 Ways to Prepare Alpo and Love It*. If you overinvest, you will keep your home mortgage too long, which will hold back the wealth-building power of your Total Money Makeover.

By the same token, do not use your potential Social Security benefits in your calculations. I don't count on an inept government for my dignity at retirement, and you shouldn't either. A recent survey said more people under age thirty believe in flying saucers than believe they will receive a dime from Social Insecurity. I tend to agree. I'm not taking a political position (although I'm not above it), but the mathematics of that system spell doom. I'm not Chicken Little predicting the sky is falling; entire books have been written on the Social Security mess. Understand, it is your job to take care of you and yours, so part of your Total Money Makeover is to invest now to make that happen. If Social Security isn't there when you retire, you'll be glad you listened to my advice. If by some miracle Social Security is there when you retire, that will mean I was wrong. In that case, you'll have some extra money to give away. I'm sure you'll forgive me for that.

Your Tool Is Mutual Funds

Now that you have reached this step, you need to learn about mutual funds. The stock market has averaged just below a 12 percent return on investment throughout its history. Growth-stock mutual funds are what I recommend investing in for the long term. Growth-stock mutual funds are lousy short-term investments because they go up and down in value, but they are excellent long-term investments when leaving the money longer than five years. One hundred percent of the fifteen-year periods in the stock market's history have made money. *The Total Money Makeover* is not an investment textbook, so if you need more detailed information, check out our class, *Financial Peace University* or my first book, *Financial Peace.* My personal retirement funds are invested the way I teach in *The Total Money Makeover.* The same was true when we were saving for our kids' college funds.

Here's a *Reader's Digest* version of my approach. I select mutual funds that have had a good track record of winning for more than five years, preferably for more than ten years. I don't look at their one-year or three-year track records because I think long term. I spread my retirement investing evenly across four types of funds. Growth and income funds get 25 percent of my investment. (They are sometimes called large cap or blue chip funds.) Growth funds get 25 percent of my investment. (They are sometimes called mid cap or equity funds; an S&P index fund would also qualify.) International funds get 25 percent of my investment. (They are sometimes called foreign or overseas funds.) Aggressive growth funds get the last 25 percent of my investment. (They are sometimes called small cap or emerging market funds.) For a full discussion of what mutual funds are and why I use this mix, go to ramseysolutions.com and search our collection of helpful articles that will give you all the info you need.

The invested 15 percent of your income should take advantage of all the matching and tax advantages available to you. Again, our purpose here is not to teach the detailed differences in every retirement plan out there (see my other materials for that), but let me give you some guidelines on where to invest first. Always start where you have a match. When your company will give you free money, take it. If your 401(k) matches the first 3 percent, the 3 percent you put in will be the first 3 percent of your 15 percent invested. If you don't have a match, or after you have invested through the match, you should next fund Roth IRAs.

The Roth IRA will allow you to invest up to $7,000 per year, per person ($8,000 if you're age 50 or older). There are some limitations as to income and situation, but most people can invest in a Roth IRA. The Roth grows tax-FREE. If you invest just $3,000 per year from age thirty-five to age sixty-five, and your mutual funds average 12 percent, you will have $873,000 tax-FREE at age sixty-five. You have invested only $90,000 (30 years x $3,000); the rest is growth, and you pay no taxes. The Roth IRA is a very important tool in virtually anyone's Total Money Makeover.

Start with any match you can get, and then fully fund Roth IRAs. Be sure the total you are putting in is 15 percent of your total household gross income. If not, go back to 401(k)s, 403(b)s, 457s, or SEPPs (for the self-employed), and invest enough so that the total invested is 15 percent of your gross annual pay.

Example:	
Household Income	**$100,000**
Husband	**$50,000**
Wife	**$50,000**
Husband's **401(k)** matches **first 3%;** wife's **401(k)** has no match	
3% of **50,000 ($1,500)** goes into the **401(k).**	
Two Roth IRAs are next, totaling **$13,500.**	
The goal is **15%** of **100,000,** which is **$15,000.**	

What It Will Take to Retire

How much do you need to retire with dignity and security? How long will it take you to get there? The investment calculator on our website (ramseysolutions.com/retirement/investment-calculator) can help give you a good estimation. You are secure and will leave a nice inheritance when you can live off of 8 percent of your nest egg per year. If you average 12 percent on your money and inflation steals 4 percent, 8 percent is a dream number. If you make 12 percent and only pull out 8 percent, you grow your nest egg by 4 percent per year. That 4 percent keeps your nest egg, and therefore your income, ahead of inflation 'til death do you part. You get a cost-of-living raise from your nest egg every year. If you can live with dignity on $60,000, you need a nest egg of only $750,000. I would recommend that you have the largest nest egg possible because there are some really cool non-greedy things to do with it later, like giving it away.

If, when you run the calculations on the worksheet, you are afraid you won't make your goal by saving 15 percent, keep in mind that this is just Baby Step Four. Later steps will allow you to accelerate your investing while still having a life.

Would you dream with me for a moment? Dream that a twenty-seven-year-old couple with average to below-average income commits to a Total Money Makeover. They get gazelle-intense, and in three years, by age thirty, they are at Step Four. They invest 15 percent of their income in four types of growth-stock mutual funds with five- to ten-year track records. The average household income in America is right around $75,000 per year, according to the Census Bureau. Joe and Suzy Average invest $11,250 (15 percent) per year, or $937.50 per month. If you make $ 75,000 per year and have no payments except the house mortgage and live on a budget, can you invest $937 per month? Follow me here. If Joe and Suzy invest $937 per month with no match into Roth IRAs from age thirty to age seventy, they will have $11 million tax-FREE! What if I'm half-wrong? What if you end up with only $5.5 million? Sure beats being one of the one in three people over age sixty who can't scrape together a thousand bucks!

I would submit to you that Joe and Suzy are well below average. Why? In our example they started at the average household income in America, and in forty years of work never got a raise. They saved 15 percent of income and never increased it by one dollar. There is no excuse to retire without financial dignity in the United States today. Most of you will have well over $3 million pass through your hands in your working lifetime, so do something about catching some of that money.

Gayle asked me one day if it was too late for her to start saving. Gayle wasn't twenty-seven like Joe and Suzy. She was fifty-seven years old, but with her attitude you would have thought this lady was 107. Harold Fisher had a much better outlook at age one hundred than Gayle did at age fifty-seven. Life had dealt her some blows and had knocked most of the hope out of her. A Total Money Makeover is not a magic show. You start where you are, and you do the steps. These steps work if you are twenty-seven or fifty-seven, and they don't change. Gayle might be starting the retirement investing step at sixty that Joe and Suzy start at thirty years old. Gayle was unwise to enter her sixties without an emergency fund and with credit-card debt and a car payment. She, like all of us, couldn't save when she has debt and no umbrella for when it rains. Would it have been better for Gayle to start when she was twenty-seven or even forty-seven? Obviously. But once she was done with the pity party, she still needed to start with Baby Step One and follow the Total Money Makeover step-by-step to put herself in the best position possible.

It is never too late to start. George Burns won his first Oscar at eighty. Golda Meir was prime minister of Israel at seventy-one. Michelangelo painted the back wall of the Sistine Chapel at sixty-six. Colonel Sanders never fried any chicken for money until he was sixty-five, and KFC (Kentucky Fried Chicken) is a household name worldwide. Albert Schweitzer was still performing surgery in Africa at eighty-nine. It is never too late to start. The past has passed. Start where you are, because that is your only option. However, a note to all of you under forty: all of us over forty are giving you a collective yell, "INVEST NOW!"

Baby Step Four is not "Get rich quick." The investing you do systematically and consistently over time will make you wealthy. If you play with this by jumping in and out, always finding something more important than investing, you are doomed to being one of those 27 out of 100 people between the ages of sixty and seventy-four still working because you have to work. Systematic, consistent investing is the tortoise that beats the hare in the race. When you keep at it, the investing compounds and explodes. The following by Timothy Gallwey always reminds me of this concept:

When we plant a rose seed in the earth, we notice it is small, but we do not criticize it as "rootless and stemless." We treat it as a seed, giving it the water and nourishment required of a seed.

When it first shoots up out of the earth, we don't condemn it as immature and underdeveloped; we do not criticize the buds for not being open when they appear. We stand in wonder at the process taking place, and give the plant the care it needs at each stage of its development.

The rose is a rose from the time it is a seed to the time it dies. Within it, at all times, it contains its whole potential. It seems to be constantly in the process of change. Yet at each state, at each moment, it is perfectly all right as it is.

A flower is not better when it blooms than when it is merely a bud; at each stage it is the same thing . . . a flower in the process of expressing its potential.

The story of the rose is about human potential and about not being defined by what you do, but rather by who you are. Your Total Money Makeover and the stage your investments are in are similar. Push with gazelle intensity to bloom, but know that as long as you take the progressive steps, *you are winning.* Ultimately, we are not defined by wealth; however, your Total Money Makeover will affect your wealth, as well as your emotions, relationships, and spiritual condition. This is a "Total" process.

I started listening to Dave a little under two years ago, and in that time we have become completely debt-free with the exception of our house! We have a fully funded emergency fund. We have two very nice vehicles, both of which are completely paid for. And, as we keep paying double toward our monthly mortgage bills, we will have our house paid off in about five years. The amazing thing is, we're only in our midtwenties!

I first got into debt before my wife and I were married. I just thought you were supposed to finance cars, and that's what I did. You can't have a car without a loan, right? At one point I was working three jobs to pay off our debt. I think the bank was wondering what in the world was going on when my car payments started coming in triple the required amount!

Once we had our entire consumer debt paid off and our emergency fund, we started investing. We used Dave's advice from *The Total Money Makeover* to invest. We have our mutual funds spread out into the four different types of funds Dave talks about—growth and income funds, growth funds, international funds, and aggressive growth funds. Thanks to Dave, our future looks very bright. If we don't earn and invest more annually than we are right now for the rest of our lives, we will still be able to retire at age sixty-five with $12 million!

It feels so good to be so young and have such financial freedom and the ability to bless other people financially. Thanks, Dave, for your financial insight and more importantly for continuing to give hope to hundreds of thousands of people.

Adam (age 24) and
Kristi (age 22) Ivey
Worship Pastor, Labor-and-Delivery
Nurse

After completing this step, you have no debt, except the house; around $10,000 cash for emergencies; and you are taking steps to make sure you will retire with dignity. I think I see a smile broadening. I know when Sharon and I reached this step, things started to move in our lives. We started to regain the confidence that losing everything had taken from us. You are going to win. Can you feel it? Can you see it? If not, go back and read that sentence again. Better yet, write it where you'll see it every day: "I am going to win!" Your life is changing! This is fun! Now, let's take another step.

Scan the QR code to see how much you should save so you can retire the way you want and find investment advisors who will create a plan to help you get there.

10

College Funding: Make Sure the Kids Are Fit Too

Time to do something about the ever-famous college fund. Many of you have been wringing your hands while we walked through four Baby Steps and have not saved so much as a dime for those little cherubs. Some people in our culture have lost their minds about college education. College is important, so important that I've explained to my kids that if they don't go to college, we will hire people to do mean things to them until they go. Seriously, a solid education to begin your adult life and your career will add to the quality of both. I also attended and graduated from college; go figure.

Understand the Purpose of a College Education Before You Fund It

I have done financial counseling for parents who I was afraid would need years of therapy if they didn't provide their children the most expensive school, free for the taking. I am sure that as we start this Baby Step, we need to examine our culture's value system on the college issue. We have sold our young people so hard and so long on college that we have begun to accept some myths about college degrees. College degrees do not ensure jobs. College degrees certainly don't ensure success. College degrees do not ensure wealth. College degrees only prove that someone has successfully passed a series of tests. We all know college-educated people who are broke and unemployed. They are very disillusioned because they thought they had bought a ticket and yet were denied a seat on the train to success.

If you are sending your kids to college because you want them to be guaranteed a job, success, or wealth, you will be dramatically let down. In some cases, the letdown won't take long because as soon as they graduate they will move back in with you. Hear me on this: college is great, but don't expect too much from that degree. What if we were to admit that, in most cases, college can only teach knowledge? If we did, we'd see that failure and heartache are guaranteed—if we expect a college degree by itself to deliver life's treasures. Only if you mix knowledge with attitude, character, perseverance, vision, diligence, and extreme levels of work will your college degree produce for you. We have placed a dangerous responsibility on that thin little sheepskin. We have asked that it do things it cannot do.

Because we have turned a college degree into some kind of "genie in a bottle" formula to help us magically win at life, we go to amazingly stupid extremes to get one. I have been a millionaire starting with nothing two times before I was forty, and I attribute 15 percent of that to college knowledge and 0 percent to the degree. The book *Emotional Intelligence* reported a similar finding. In studying successful people, the author discovered that 15 percent of success could be attributed to training and education, while 85 percent was attributed to attitude, perseverance, diligence, and vision. If we admit out loud that education is for knowledge, which is only part of the formula to success, then we don't have to lose our minds in pursuit of the Holy Grail degree.

What about those lifelong friends your children will make in college who can "help" them when they graduate? Let me ask you: Have you made any extra money because of friendships you made in college? I'm not saying friendships don't matter, or even that college friends won't ever help you in your career; however, if the price for those kinds of friendships is major debt, it's way too high. Besides, you can build quality relationships for the future no matter where you attend school.

We need this foundation of why we want college for our kids in order to set goals for school. In other words, if you do not expect quite as much from the degree, maybe you won't break all the branches in your family tree getting the kids into a college you frankly can't afford. Again, college is important—very important—but it is not the answer to all your kids' problems. I will be so bold as to say college isn't even a need; it is a want. It isn't a necessity; it is a luxury. This luxury is one of the first on my list, but not before retirement, not before an emergency fund, and certainly not as a reason to go into debt.

DAVE RANTS...

One Myth About the College Degree

I've never walked into a doctor's office and said, "You know what, Doc, before you check my blood pressure, you better tell me where you went to medical school." And I've never gone into my CPA's office and quizzed him about where he got his accounting degree.

But when we're picking a school for ourselves or our kids, we act like where we get our degree is some kind of magical fairy dust that's going to automatically make our lives successful. Here's a shocker: it's not.

Knowledge, perseverance, integrity, and character will carry you a lot farther than a piece of paper with a particular school's logo on it. When I hire team members at my company, I almost never look at where they went to school. I care more about what they've done since they left there.

Now, I'm not against an elite education or a private education. But what I am against is the debt that usually comes with those degrees and the lack of thought that often goes into getting them.

People call my radio show all the time with $100,000 in student loans while work-ing a job that brings in $58,000 a year. That math just doesn't work, and people just can't live that way—especially when a spouse and family come along. And it's getting worse, with the grand total of all student loan debt in America now at $1.7 trillion!

Bottom line: the most useless part of your *degree* is its *pedigree*. To be finan-cially successful, you've got to quit caring about what other people think. If you can really *get* that before you go to college, then you're making a giant step in the right direction.

Dave's Rules for College

Do some research on the cost of attending college. Find out what your old college costs today. Find out what the big state school in your area costs. Find out what the smaller state school in your neighborhood costs. Find out what the private, smaller, more intimate college costs. Compare them. In some areas of study and in a very few careers, where you gradu-ate from will matter, but in most it won't. Pedigree means less and less in our work culture today. How can you justify going into debt $75,000 for a degree when you could have gone to a state school and paid for it out of your pocket debt-free? You can't. If you have the $75,000 extra cash or a free-ride scholarship and want to go to that private school debt-free, by all means, do it. Otherwise, reconsider.

The first rule of college (whether for you or for your children) is: pay cash. The second rule is: if you have the cash or the scholarship, go. A couple of years ago I met with the dean of the college of business from the university where I graduated. At that time, the average college student graduated with about $30,000 in student-loan debt after spending four years in an apartment, not the dorm, and eating off-campus, not on the meal plan. The average student paid $6,500 *more per year* to live and eat off-campus than to live in the dorm and eat cafeteria food. The student loans that they "had to have" or they wouldn't be able to go to college weren't for college at all. The bulk of the student loans, on average, paid for an off-campus standard of living, and almost no debt went to pay for the actual degree, only to look good while getting the degree.

Student loans are a cancer. Once you have them, you can't get rid of them. They are like an unwelcome relative who comes to stay for a "few days" and is still in the guest room ten years later. We have spread the myth that you can't be a student without a loan. Not true! According to *US News*, two out of three college students take out student loans. Student loans have become normal, and normal is broke. In fact, the current generation of students is sometimes nicknamed "Generation Debt" because they're graduating from four-year schools with an average of $37,000 in student loan debt. Stay away from loans; make plans to avoid borrowing.

If you've planned your savings goals and don't have much room in the budget for college, don't panic. Knowledge is just part of the formula to success. With what you are able to save, those precious kids can probably get a good degree if they will suffer through lifestyle adjustments and get a job while in school. Work is good for them. In past generations, students lived with relatives, slept in dorms, ate cafeteria food, and endured other hardships to get a degree. They even went to schools without pedigrees to get the knowledge, which is what they were after. They also were under no illusions of the degree giving them guaranteed jobs or success.

Now, after spending pages harping on mindset, we can set some reasonable, attainable goals for saving for college.

Baby Step Five: Save for Your Children's College Fund

Virtually everyone thinks saving for college is important, but hardly anyone saves money for their kids' college education. BestColleges.com found that 44 percent of Americans with kids don't save a dime toward college. According to a 2022 study by Sallie Mae, only 33 percent of families use college savings funds like educational savings accounts (ESAs) and

529 plans. Why are we doing so badly? Because we are in debt, have no emergency savings, no budget, and so on. We have to Baby-Step our way here in our Total Money Makeover before we have the money to save for college. If you save for college and don't have an emergency fund, you will raid the college fund to keep the home out of foreclosure when you get laid off. If you try to save for college while making payments on everything under the sun, you won't have any money to save. On the other hand, by the time you get here in the Baby Steps, you'll have a strong foundation and money to save. If you don't have children, or your kids are grown and gone, you will simply skip this step. For everyone else, a college fund is a necessity. And if you do what I say, when you do start a college fund, you won't end up raiding it.

When we first started looking at college options for our daughter, we got really worried. We always lived within our means, but we never saved for the future. We've heard of students racking up tens of thousands of dollars in debt for college, but we didn't want our daughter to have that burden when she finished her education.

We didn't think it was possible to pay cash for college. At first, we just thought we would help her as much as possible with what we had, and then we'd go into debt to cover the rest of the expenses.

With a little research, we found that our daughter could get most of her classes done at a community college—and for a lot less! She drove twenty miles each way for two years and was able to live at home. Best of all, she won three different scholarships, which paid for half of her tuition!

After two years, she graduated with an associate's degree in art and transferred to a four-year college. She worked hard and received even more scholarships, which lowered her tuition bill. We helped by paying her apartment rent and tuition, and she worked part-time to pay for books, food, and living expenses. This was an exercise in teamwork, and we all stayed focused on the goal: graduating with no debt.

We discovered that with a little creativity and a lot of hard work, we really could pay cash for our daughter's education—and it worked! Our daughter will graduate in a few months with no student loans!

Craig (age 55) and
Karen (age 52) Seymour
Optician; Police Department Records

ESAs and 529s

College tuition goes up faster than regular inflation. Inflation of goods and services averages about 4 percent per year, while tuition inflation averages about 8 percent per year. When you save for college, you have to make at least 8 percent per year to keep up with the increases. Baby life insurance, like Gerber or other whole life for babies to save for college, is a joke—it usually takes around 15 years for the cash value of those plans to equal the amount you've paid in premiums. That's just ridiculous. Savings bonds won't work either (sorry, Grandma!) because they average between 2 and 5 percent. Most states now offer prepaid college tuition. We discussed that in chapter four on money myths, but remember that when you prepay anything, you simply break even with inflation on that item. If tuition goes up 8 percent a year and you prepay it, you make 8 percent on your money. That is not too bad, but keep in mind that a decent growth-stock mutual fund will average over 12 percent when invested long term. Of course, there are worse things than prepaid tuition. BestColleges.com reports that 22 percent of the few who actually save for college do so in a simple savings account yielding less than 1 percent. That won't get it done. I know, something's better than nothing. But I like another adage better in this case: if something's worth doing, it's worth doing right. Let's do Baby Step Five the right way.

I suggest funding college, or at least the first step of college, with an ESA, funded in a growth-stock mutual fund. The educational savings account, nicknamed the education IRA, grows tax-free when used for higher education. If you invest $2,000 a year from birth to age eighteen in prepaid tuition, that would purchase about $72,000 in tuition, but through an ESA in mutual funds averaging 12 percent, you would have $126,000 tax-free. The ESA currently allows you to invest $2,000 per year, per child, if your household income is under $190,000 per year. The investment limit drops gradually with higher incomes, and anyone earning over $220,000 is ineligible. If you start investing early, your child can go to virtually any state college for four years if you save $166.67 per month ($2,000/year). For most of you, Baby Step Five is handled if you start fully funding an ESA by the time your child is five or under.

If your children are older, or you have aspirations of expensive schools, graduate school, or PhD programs that you pay for, you will have to save more than the ESA will allow. I would still start with the ESA if the income limits don't keep you out. Start with the ESA because you can invest it anywhere, in any fund or any mix of funds, and change it at will. It is the most flexible, and you have the most control.

If you want to do more than the ESA, or your income rules you out, you may want to look at a 529 plan. These are state plans, but most allow you to use the money at any institution of higher learning, which means you can save in New Hampshire's 529 plan and go to college in Kansas. There are several types of 529 plans, and you should stay away from most of them. The first type to become popular was the "life phase" plan. This type of plan allows the plan administrator to control your money and move it to more conservative investments as the child ages. These perform poorly (at about 8 percent) because they are very conservative. The next type is a "prepaid" plan, which lets you prepay for future college expenses at the current tuition rates. We've already talked about the problems with anything prepaid, but these prepaid plans have even more. Prepaid 529 plans have strict eligibility requirements and put a bunch of restrictions on how you can use the funds.

One of the problems with a 529 plan is that you must give up an element of control. The best 529 plans available, and my second choice to an ESA, is a "flexible" plan. This type of plan allows you to move your investment around periodically within a certain family of funds. A family of funds is a brand name of mutual fund. You could pick from virtually any mutual fund in the American Funds Group or Vanguard or Fidelity. You are stuck in one brand, but you can choose the type of fund, the amount in each, and move it around if you want. This is the only type of 529 I recommend.

Regardless of how you save for college, do it. Saving for college ensures that a legacy of debt is not passed down your family tree. Sadly, most people graduating from college right now are deeply in debt before they start their careers. If you start early or save aggressively, your child will not be one of them.

After being tired and frustrated with compiling debt over several years, I was ready to free myself and start planning for a better future. My not-yet-husband, Jared, was a great encourager, but it made all the difference when my sister told me about Dave. Jared and I read *The Total Money Makeover*, attended a Live Event, and decided it was time to attack our debt with gazelle intensity before we got married.

Each of us paid off our cars. Jared finally was able to get rid of his $36,000 in student loans, and together we were able to save $9,000 for our wedding. It was nice being newlyweds with a budget and a financial plan. Once we didn't have credit cards to tempt us to make silly purchases, sticking to the budget and saving money became so much easier. Also, we each allotted ourselves a certain amount of money that we could use however we wanted. We chose to save most of it, which curbed buying things impulsively too. Since we were making about $42,000 a year, we had to be smart with our purchases, and we decided to buy used furniture and trade in my SUV for a more economical car.

Not living paycheck to paycheck is a great feeling. Jared and I are on the same page financially, and we are very excited about our future. It's a great feeling to be planning for what's ahead of you instead of having to pay off your past. We are currently building up our emergency fund and saving up for a down payment on a house. When we finally decide where we want to settle down, it will be nice to have the money to make the change!

**Vaneesa (age 30) and
Jared (age 28) Smith**
Server, Chef

Getting Creative When You Don't Have Much Time

What if you have only a couple of years and will not be able to save much because you started your Total Money Makeover later in life? First, revisit the concepts at the beginning of the chapter. Plan on your child attending somewhere that is cheaper, living on campus, and eating the cafeteria food. Knowledge is what you are after, not a pedigree. Student loans are off-limits. You must get creative and resourceful. Have your children think of companies that might be looking to hire someone with the degree they want. Have them ask the company to pay their way through school while they work for them. Many companies pay tuition for their "adult" employees; just reverse it on them. Will they all say yes? Absolutely not; in fact, most will say no, but it only takes one yes, so ask often.

Look into companies that have work-study programs. Many companies offer to pay for school and have struck tuition deals with local colleges to attract a labor force. Disney, for instance, has a program where you can get your tuition paid up front and get your books reimbursed after ninety days of employment—and that includes both full- and part-time jobs. That is just one example of many. This type of program is for someone who wants the knowledge, not to go to school just for the "college experience," which translates into: they want to party. If you want to go into debt to teach your kids to drink beer or for them to get a pedigree, you need more than a simple Total Money Makeover.

Look into what the military has to offer. The military isn't for everyone, but a young man who used to work for me got a free college education by serving four years in the army. Honestly, he hated the army, but it was his ticket to school. He grew up in subsidized housing and was told all his life that college was not in his future. He just wouldn't be denied.

I was at the end of my rope, robbing Peter to pay Paul. I had maxed out two credit cards and had no more "wiggle room." I knew that I couldn't keep it up much longer.

I was looking at $35,000 worth of debt—and I only made $35,000 a year in income! When my car broke down and the mechanic gave me a $1,500 estimate on repairs, something had to give!

First, I shopped around and found a good mechanic to do the work for just $300. Then, I took a second job to pay for it.

Soon after, I finally decided to attack my debt once and for all. I wanted to do it fast, so I got extra jobs. I spent ten hours a day on Saturdays and Sundays cleaning rooms at a fancy resort. I remember driving from my second job and crying because I didn't want to scrub toilets or make beds anymore! But I knew it would be worth it in the end.

It was tough, but I did it—I paid off all $35,000 in debt! I got rid of all my credit cards and stopped buying useless stuff. Plus, I have an emergency fund and a new-car fund. Having a plan for my money changed my life! People made fun of me when I was working two or three jobs at a time, but now I'm debt-free and ahead of the game!

Shelley Hogenhout (age 31)
Business Process Improvement
Analyst

If full-time military service isn't for you, check out the National Guard. They will pay you to go to boot camp one summer between high school and college and will then pay for enough tuition and books to get you through the rest of the time. Of course, you will serve your country in the National Guard.

Take a high-rejection, high-paying summer sales job. There are countless stories of young people selling books or participating in similar programs to get through school. Some of these young guerrilla-combat salespeople get more of an education in the summer trenches than they do in marketing class. A friend of mine made $40,000 selling in one summer. Upon returning to class in the fall, his marketing professor gave him a C on a sales presentation he did in front of the class. My friend, being immature, asked the professor what he made a year. After some goading, the professor admitted to an income of $35,000 per year. My friend walked out and, sadly, he quit school. He will be okay, though; his income last year was over $1,200,000. I don't tell the story to say it is good to be immature and quit school, because even he would tell you he wishes he had finished. I tell that true story because it illustrates that he learned very valuable lessons about marketing while trying to pay for school. There are benefits beyond just the money awaiting the young person who works to pay for all or part of college.

If you already have the student loans or don't want to get a loan in the first place, look into the "underserved areas" programs. The government agrees to pay your student loans if you serve in a rural or inner-city area. This is mostly for students graduating with law, medicine, nursing, or teaching degrees. But make sure you're not getting tangled up in a Public Service Loan Forgiveness Program where the government is supposed to forgive student loan debt for people who work for certain employers for a certain amount of time. That program has been a massive disappointment, forgiving debt for just a tiny fraction of the people who have applied.

Probably my favorite method of funding school, other than saving for it, is scholarships. There is a dispute as to how many scholarships go unclaimed every year. Certainly there are people on the Internet who will hype you on this subject. However, legitimately there are hundreds of millions of dollars in scholarships given out every year. These scholarships are not just academic or athletic scholarships either. They are of small- to medium-sized dollar amounts from organizations like community clubs. The Rotary Club, the Lions Club, or the Jaycees many times have $250 or $500 per year they award to some good young citizen. Some of these scholarships are based on race or sex or religion. For instance, they might be designed to help someone with Native American heritage get an education.

The lists of these scholarships can be found through free, online scholarship search tools and databases and the Free Application for Federal Student Aid (FAFSA). Denise, a listener to my show, took my advice, filled out the FAFSA, and searched for other scholarships online. Her search results covered more than 300,000 available scholarships, which she filtered for her situation, interests, and education. This narrowed down the list to 1,000 to apply for. She spent the whole summer filling out applications and writing essays. She literally applied for 1,000 scholarships. Denise was turned down by 970, but was awarded 30 scholarships, and those paid her $38,000. With the additional $8,000 in scholarships she received from her school by filling out the FAFSA, she ended up with more than enough to cover her tuition for all four years while her next-door neighbor sat and whined that no money was available for school and eventually got a student loan.

If you walk your way up these Baby Steps, you can send your kids to school without debt. Even if you start late, perseverance and resourcefulness can get them through school. If you want to go to college badly enough in America today, you can. The good news is that those of you who have a Total Money Makeover will likely not only pay for your child's education, but also—by teaching your children to handle money, and by becoming wealthy—your grandchildren can go to school debt-free.

Scan this QR code to find out how important school choice is to the success of your debt-free college plan. You have options!

And, if you want to get ahead of college costs, talk with an investment advisor. They can help you understand your options for college savings plans and make informed investing decisions. Scan the QR code to find advisors near you.

11

Pay Off the Home Mortgage: Be Ultra-Fit

I have a good friend who runs a lot of marathons. I sit and listen in awe to the stories of all the marathons he has run. I am amazed by the dedication, training, and pain marathoners embrace. I have personally run one full marathon, and I enjoy doing several half marathons a year, but these folks who do multiple marathons every year are some of the fittest people in the world. As you reach Baby Step Six (Pay Off Your Home Early), you reach marathoner status in the wealth-building world. You have run the good race, but you aren't done.

Bruce, my marathon friend, told me (and I experienced it too) that at about the eighteen-mile mark (out of 26.2), runners begin to lock up. Some really nasty things start to happen to your muscles and your mind at that point. You're almost through the race and nothing wants you to finish. The highly trained and conditioned body starts talking to you about stopping. Big black clouds of doubt enter the mentally tough and trained competitive mind. You begin to think things like, *Eighteen miles is pretty good; few others could accomplish that*. If you aren't really careful, "The Good Enough" can become the enemy of "The Best."

"Bad" is seldom the enemy of "The Best," but mediocrity with a dose of doubt can keep you from excellence. Finishing well can be more important than starting well.

Reach for the Gold Ring

At this point in your Total Money Makeover, you are debt-free except for the house, and you have three to six months of expenses ($15,000+/–) saved for emergencies. At this point in your Total Money Makeover, you are putting 15 percent of your income into retirement savings and you are investing for your kid's college education with firm goals in sight on both. You are now one of the top 5 to 10 percent of Americans because you have some wealth, have a plan, and are under control. At this point in your Total Money Makeover, you are in grave danger! You are in danger of settling for "Good Enough." You are at the eighteen-mile mark of a marathon, and now that it is time to reach for the really big gold ring, the final two Baby Steps could seem out of your reach. Let me assure you that many have been at this point. Some have stopped and regretted it; others have stayed gazelle-intense long enough to finish the race. The latter have looked and seen just one major hurdle left, after which they can walk with pride among the ultra-fit who call themselves financial marathoners. They can count themselves among the elite who have finished the Total Money Makeover.

We started Dave's plan for a Total Money Makeover in 2002 with over $3,000 in a home equity loan, credit-card bills, a $30,000 mortgage, and no emergency fund or savings. We were living on about $45,000 and felt out of control. When we learned about the Baby Step process, we knew that it was the best way out. We started working through the Baby Steps as quickly as we could, and our lives began an immediate change.

We knew we had to first get on a budget and get that debt snowball going. The best way to jump-start things was to have a garage sale. It was great! We made over $500 and paid off quite a few bills immediately. We continued to work and save and work some more. We were determined to beat the system and press forward. We paid off the consumer debt, fully funded our emergency fund, and started investing. We were amazed with how focused we had become on getting completely out of debt.

But we didn't stop there—the ultimate challenge was to pay off the house. This was one of the most challenging things I've ever done in my whole life. I got a second part-time job cleaning offices thirty hours a week in addition to working full-time. Joe worked overtime seven days a week. For five grueling months we worked harder than we ever had in our entire lives, but we knew that it was worth it. And then, finally, in September of 2005, we reached our goal. We paid off our house, making us completely DEBT-FREE!!!

It's unbelievable the feeling of freedom that comes when you don't have the weight of payments hanging over your head. We can now focus on saving for retirement entirely and start really living! I even got to quit my job and start my own business so I don't have to go to a dreaded J-O-B every day; I get to do what I love. Good things really do come to those who wait.

God has definitely blessed us through this experience. For the first time, our future plans won't just seem like a dream, but we can make them a reality. If we can do this, anyone can!

**Carla (age 38) and
Joe (age 43) Schubeck**
Designer/Minister; Press Operator

Baby Step Six: Pay Off Your Home Early

The final hurdle before you turn the corner for the last few miles is to become completely debt-free. No payments. How would it feel to have no payments? I have said it before, and I will repeat myself until you hear me: if you invested what you pay in monthly payments, you'd be a debt-free millionaire before long. Your largest wealth-building tool is your income; you have read that over and over. Now you get to see the possibilities unfold. You have trained, conditioned, and eaten right to run this marathon, so don't quit on the eighteenth mile! Every dollar in your budget that you can find above living, retirement, and college should be used to make extra payments on your home. Attack that home mortgage with gazelle intensity.

My family had a fabulous dog, a Chinese pug, a dog like Frank in the *Men in Black* movies. Her name was Heaven, and when we talked to her, she cocked her little round head sideways in a questioning look as if we'd lost our minds. If you heard the way we talked to the dog, you might think we really had lost our minds. We have all seen the cocked-sideways look coming at us when we have said something weird, something against the culture. When I say, "Pay off the mortgage," some of you look at this book as if I had told you to build wings and fly to the moon.

Anytime I speak about paying off mortgages, people give me that special look. They think I'm crazy for two reasons. One, most people have lost their hope, and they don't really believe there is any chance for them. Two, most people believe all the mortgage myths that have been spread. Yes, we must dispel a few more myths. There are two really big "reasons" that keep seemingly intelligent people (like me for years) from paying off mortgages, so we will start with those.

Remember, Beware of the Myths

Big Reason Number One:

MYTH: It is wise to keep my home mortgage to get the tax deduction.

TRUTH: Tax deductions are no bargain.

We discussed tax-deduction math when we looked at car fleeces. Let's review. If you have a home with a payment of around $1,500, and the interest portion is $900 per month, you have paid around $10,000 in interest that year, which creates a tax deduction. If, instead, you have a debt-free home, you would, in fact, lose the tax deduction, so the myth says to keep your home mortgaged because of tax advantages.

This situation is one more opportunity to discover if your CPA can add. If you do not have a $10,000 tax deduction and you are in a 22 percent bracket, you will have to pay $2,200 in taxes on that $10,000. According to the myth, we should send $10,000 in interest to the bank so we don't have to send $2,200 in taxes to the IRS. Personally, I think I will live debt-free and not make a $10,000 trade for $2,200. However, any of you who want $2,200 of your taxes paid, just email me and I will personally pay $2,200 of your taxes as soon as your check for $10,000 clears into my bank account. I can add.

DAVE RANTS . . .

If you get a big tax refund, you've just allowed the government to use your money interest-free for one year.

Big Reason Number Two:

MYTH: It is wise to borrow all I can on my home (or continually refinance for cash out) because the interest rate is lower than the return I can get if I invest the money.

TRUTH: You really don't make anything when the smoke clears.

This one is a little complicated, but if you follow me, you will have intellectually grasped why so many people have fallen into a financial pit. The myth that I was taught in academia (I am not against higher learning, by the way, as long as we are learning the truth) is to use lower-interest debt to invest in higher-return investments. Sadly, some "financial planners" have told Americans to borrow on their homes at around 8 percent to invest in good growth-stock mutual funds averaging around 12 percent because you make an easy 4 percent spread.

Mutual funds are awesome investments, and as I have said, I personally have tons of money invested in good growth-stock mutual funds. Also, the stock market has averaged around 12 percent from the beginning. Some years are great and some are lousy, and we have had both in the last ten years, but the long-term average is around 12 percent. So I buy and recommend mutual funds.

The problem with this myth is that the assumptions used to get to that 4 percent spread or profit on investing are wrong. Mythsayers, and I have been one, are very naive in how they approach investing.

Let's look at borrowing $100,000 on your home to invest. If you borrowed at 8 percent, you would pay $8,000 in interest, and if you invested the $100,000 you borrowed on your home and made 12 percent, you would make $12,000 in return, netting you $4,000. Or would you? Where I live, if you make $12,000 on an investment, you will pay taxes. If you are in a 22 percent bracket, you will pay $2,600 in taxes at ordinary income rates or $1,500 if you invest at capital gains rates. So you will not net $4,000, but instead $1,400 to $2,500. But we aren't through yet.

If I own the home next to you and have no debt, and you (because of your investment adviser guy) borrowed $100,000 on your home, who has taken more risk? When the economy moves south, when there is war or rumors of war, when you get sick or have a car wreck or are downsized, you will run into major problems with a $100,000 mortgage that I will never have. So debt causes risk to increase.

I can prove to you that risk increases. With the drop in real estate values and the slowing market in the 2008–09 recession, many people lost their homes to foreclosure. I have done in-depth, detailed research and have found that 100 percent of the foreclosed homes had a mortgage. Ha! Sadly, some of the people who lost their homes had a naive financial planner who left risk out of his formula and suggested they "harvest" their equity. Like Warren Buffet said, "When the tide goes out, you can tell who was skinny-dipping."

Since debt causes increased risk, we must mathematically factor in a reduction in return if we are sophisticated investors. If you can make around 12 percent on a mutual fund, and I try to get you to invest in a bet on the roulette wheel, which will return you 500 percent, you would automatically say the two don't compare. Why? Risk. Common sense tells you not to compare mutual funds and roulette wheel returns without adjusting the returns for risk. Common sense tells you to discount the 500 percent upside of the roulette wheel because of risk. After discounting the roulette wheel for risk, you would rather have the mutual fund. Good choice.

Actually, this is done in academia as well. There is a statistical measure of risk called a beta. A big beta means a big risk. Graduate-level financial people who are taught mathematical formulas to make risky investments compare apples to apples with safer investments after adjustment for risk. We just never apply that formula to a debt-free home versus a mortgaged and invested home, which is very naive. The technical formula is great for putting you to sleep, but understand that you can't compare risk with no risk unless you make adjustments.

The bottom line is that after adjusting for taxes and risk, you don't make money on our little formula. Throughout a lifetime of investing and mortgaging, the debt-free person will actually come out ahead.

MYTH: Take out a thirty-year mortgage and promise yourself to pay it like a fifteen-year, so if something goes wrong you have wiggle room.

TRUTH: Something will go wrong.

One thing I am sure of in my Total Money Makeover: I had to quit telling myself that I had innate discipline and fabulous natural self-control. That is a lie. I have to put systems and programs in place that make me do smart things. Saying "Cross my fingers and hope to die, I promise, promise, promise I will pay extra on my mortgage because I am the one human on the planet who has that kind of discipline" is kidding yourself. A big part of being strong financially is that you know where you are weak and take action to make sure you don't fall prey to the weakness. And we ALL are weak.

Sick children, bad transmissions, prom dresses, high heat bills, and dog vaccinations come up, and you won't make the extra payment. Then we extend the lie by saying, "Oh, I will next month." Grow up! Research has found that almost no one systematically monthly pays extra on their mortgage; you simply can't kid yourself.

Shorter Terms Matter	
Purchase Price	$495,000
Down Payment	$49,500
Mortgage Amount	$445,500

At 7% Interest Rate		
30 Years	$2,964	$1,067,014
15 Years	$4,004	$720,770
Difference	$1,040	$346,244

For a payment of $1,040 more per month you will save almost $350,000 and fifteen years of bondage. The really interesting thing I have observed is that fifteen-year mortgages always pay off in fifteen years. Again, part of a Total Money Makeover is putting in place systems that automate smart moves, which is what a fifteen-year mortgage is. Thirty-year mortgages are for people who enjoy slavery so much they want to extend it for fifteen more years and pay hundreds of thousands of dollars more for the privilege. If you must take out a mortgage, pretend only fifteen-year mortgages exist.

If you have a great interest rate, it is not necessary to refinance to pay a mortgage off in fifteen years or earlier. Simply make payments as if you have a fifteen-year mortgage, and your mortgage will pay off in fifteen years. If you want to pay any mortgage off in twelve years or any number you want, visit my website or get a calculator and calculate the proper payment at your interest rate on your balance for a twelve-year mortgage (or the number you want). Once you have that payment amount, add to your monthly mortgage payment the difference between the new principal and interest payment and your current principal and interest payment, and you will pay off your home in twelve years.

The best time to refinance is when you can save on interest. Use the calculators on my website at ramseysolutions.com/tools to determine whether you should refinance. When refinancing, paying points or origination fees is not in your best interest. Points or origination fees are prepaid interest. When you pay points, you get a lower annual percentage rate (APR) because you have already paid some of the interest up front. The math shows that you don't save enough on interest rates to pay yourself back for the points. When you pay points, you are prepaying interest, and it takes an average of about ten years to get your money back. Freddie Mac says the median life of a mortgage is a little more than three years, so on average you don't save enough to get your money back before you pay the loan off by moving or refinancing. When refinancing, ask for a "par" quote, which means zero points and zero origination fee. The mortgage broker can make a profit by selling the loan; they don't need the origination fee to be profitable.

MYTH: It is wise to use the lower rates offered by an ARM mortgage or balloon mortgage if you know you'll "be moving in a few years anyway."

TRUTH: You will be moving when they foreclose.

The ARM, adjustable rate mortgage, was invented in the early 1980s. Prior to that, those of us in the real estate business sold fixed-rate 7 or 8 percent mortgages. What happened? I was there in the middle of that disaster of an economy when fixed-rate mortgages went as high as 17 percent and the real estate world froze. Lenders paid out 12 percent on CDs but had money loaned out at 7 percent on hundreds of millions of dollars in mortgages. They were losing money, and lenders don't like to lose money. So the adjustable rate mortgage was born, in which your interest rate goes up when the prevailing market interest rates go up. The ARM was born to transfer the risk of higher interest rates to you, the consumer. Over the last several years, home mortgage rates held steady at historic lows. At the time of this writing, rates have swung back up to twenty-year highs. It is not wise to get something that adjusts when you are at the bottom of rates! Nor should you sign up for that ride when rates are trending upward. The mythsayers always seem to want to add risk to your home, the one place you should want to make sure has stability.

Balloon mortgages are even worse. Balloons pop, and it is always strange to me that the popping sound is so startling. Why don't we expect it? It is in the very nature of balloons to pop. Wise financial people always move away from risk, and the balloon mortgage creates risk nightmares. When your entire mortgage is due in thirty-six or sixty months, you send out engraved invitations for Murphy (Remember him? If it can go wrong, it will) to live in your spare bedroom. I have seen hundreds of clients and callers like Jill over the years.

Jill is the wife of a sophisticated, upwardly mobile corporate guy. Her husband assured her they would be moving up because his career was on the fast track. So they got the lower interest rate and took a five-year balloon. "We just knew we would move inside five years," she said. Her husband began having headaches in the third year of the mortgage, which, sadly, they discovered were caused by a brain tumor. We met this upwardly mobile corporate executive with limited speech and in a wheel-chair, totally and permanently disabled at thirty-eight years of age. His life had been spared, but the surgeries had devastated him. Jill, now a middle-aged mom of two with a disabled husband, didn't have the income to refinance the home when the balloon came due.

The bank wasn't evil; they were just doing their job as they began fore-closure. I wish I could tell you a happy ending, but the truth is, they sold their home at a deep discount to stop the foreclosure and now rent and try to survive. All of this happened because they tried to save a few dollars on the interest rate, "and we knew we were going to move." They did.

MYTH: A home equity loan is good to have instead of an emergency fund.

TRUTH: Again, emergencies are precisely when you don't need debt.

The home equity loan or home equity line of credit is one of the most aggressively marketed loans today. The average American in debt to his eyeballs has exhausted all means of borrowing except the big second mortgage on his home. This is very sad because we now put our homes at risk to go on vacation, open a business, consolidate debt, or just for an emergency fund. Families come to us in dire straits when the home equity loan is their last bad mistake and the straw that breaks the camel's back.

The banking industry calls these loans HELs for short, and my experience tells me they simply left off an *L*. These loans are very dangerous, and an unbelievable amount of them end in foreclosure.

Even a conservative person who doesn't have credit-card debt and pays cash for vacations can make the mistake of the HEL by setting up a loan or a "line of credit" (called a HELOC) just for emergencies. That seems reasonable until you have walked through an emergency or two, and you realize very plainly that an emergency is the last time you need to be borrowing money. If you have a car wreck or lose your job and then borrow $30,000 against your home to live on while you make a comeback, you will likely lose your home. Most HELs are renewable annually, meaning they requalify you for the loan once a year.

Ed and Sally didn't realize this. Ed is a very sophisticated financial guy, or so he thought, so he had a HEL for emergencies. Sally had a bad car wreck, and within three months Ed got downsized. They quickly went through the HEL and then got behind in their bills. The annual renewal came up on the HEL, and the bank chose not to renew their loan because of their bad credit, which had been perfect for the previous seventeen years of marriage. The bank called the note. Ed couldn't believe the bank would kick them when they were down. The note being called meant they had to refinance to pay off the bank, but guess what? They couldn't because their credit was bad. The end result was very sad; they sold their home to avoid a foreclosure. Ed was wrong. They should have had an emergency fund instead of a loan.

MYTH: You can't pay cash for a home!

TRUTH: Bet me.

First, let me tell you that mortgage debt is the only kind of debt I don't yell about. I want you to pay off your home as a part of your Total Money Makeover, and, for all the reasons stated in the previous pages, you have to be very careful. When asked about mortgages, I tell everyone never to take more than a fifteen-year fixed-rate loan, and never have a payment of over 25 percent of your take-home pay. That is the most you should ever borrow.

I don't borrow money—ever. Luke called me from Cleveland to tell me that some of our listeners and readers are doing what Sharon and I have done, "The 100-Percent-Down Plan." Pay cash. Most people don't think that can be done. Luke did it.

Luke made really good money. His income at twenty-three years old was $65,000, and he married a young lady making $40,000. His grand-father had preached to him never to borrow money. So Luke and his new bride lived in a very small apartment over a rich lady's garage. They paid only $500 a month for it. They lived on nothing, did nothing that cost money, and they saved. Man, did they save! Making over $100,000 in the household, they saved $70,000 a year for three years and paid cash for a $200,000 home. They closed on the home on Luke's wife's twenty-sixth birthday. They lived like no one else, and now they are living like no one else. If you make $100,000 per year and don't have any payments, you can become very wealthy very quickly. Keep in mind, though, that Luke's friends and relatives thought he should be committed. They made fun of his cars, his lifestyle, and his dream. Only his bride and his grandfather believed in his dream. Who cares what the broke people think?

You may not make $105,000 per year, but you may not need a $200,000 home as your starter either. You may not make $105,000 per year, so your dream might take five years instead of three, like Luke's. Ask any eighty-year-old if five years of sacrifice is worth it to change your financial destiny for the rest of your life! Ask any eighty-year-old if five years of sacrifice is worth it to have the satisfaction of knowing you changed your family tree. Paying cash for a home is possible, very possible. What's hard to find is people willing to pay the price in sacrificed lifestyle.

Before we got married, Doug and I had both been divorced and both had custody of our children. As single parents, it was a struggle to afford house payments and all the other bills associated with everyday life. Every time the mortgage or rent was due, the checkbook got tighter and tighter. I was trying to finish college, and he had a lot of unpaid debt from his previous marriage. I had one credit card that I found myself using for emergencies (car repairs, etc.). I didn't believe in carrying a balance on it, but our debt was fairly substantial when we got married.

Shortly into our marriage, we began our Total Money Makeover. Doug listened to the radio show every day during his thirty-minute commute to work and was convinced of the financial peace we could have in our future by simply following the Baby Steps. I decided to get onboard with him, because we really had nothing left to lose at this point.

After we stopped using our credit cards, we spent a lot less! And establishing a budget highlighted the areas in which we had been blindly wasting our money. We realized a lot of our expenses were due to eating out and various luxury items that we could live without. We decided to take every extra dollar we had and pay off our credit card. Next we paid off my car. Then we set up our emergency fund and began working on our mortgage. Thankfully, we paid off the house a year and a half ahead of schedule! While so many people don't even realize the importance and sense of fulfillment that come from owning your home, we found this to be the last and biggest step in finding true financial peace.

Since we've become debt-free, we have greatly enjoyed taking more family vacations and spending time together. There is so much less stress on the entire family! It's amazing how much easier it was to bring the family closer together once we eliminated all the money concerns we used to have. We still do not live lavishly, and we love to bargain shop for everything we buy, but the peace we have from being debt-free is worth the small sacrifices! Thanks for redirecting the course our family was headed down, Dave!

**Sabrina (age 42) and
Doug (age 52) Howerton**
*Retail-Store Manager, Aluminum Mill
Worker*

A Picture of Freedom

Well, there it is, Baby Step Six, debt-free and loving it. Our observation of families who stay gazelle-intense is that they pay off the mortgage about seven years from the date they declared war on the culture, from the date they decided to have a Total Money Makeover. I'm sure by now you are reassured that this is not a get-rich-quick book. What kind of author would tell a microwave culture that it takes an average of seven years to reach the last Baby Step? What kind of author would tell a sound-bite culture that the first two steps take a very tough two or two and a half years? An author who has seen it done tens of thousands of times by ordinary people with extraordinary desire would do that, the same author who tells you it's not easy, just worth it.

I have used the emotional tag with radio audiences and live audiences that the grass will feel different under your feet when you own it. When you pay off the mortgage, have a barefoot mortgage-burning party and invite all your friends, relatives, and neighbors. Maybe they will catch the bug and want a Total Money Makeover when they see yours is really working.

Over the years, people have sent me all kinds of mementos from their Total Money Makeover. Many of them are creative uses of destroyed and maimed credit cards sent in by folks who have discovered if they will live like no one else, later they can live like no one else. One of the more memorable gifts I received came in a Ziploc bag—accompanied by a letter. This letter and sample of fescue were handed to me in person in a shopping mall in Louisville, Kentucky. I was there doing a radio appearance and book signing when up walked Alicia, or "Al," as she likes to be called.

According to her letter, Al's story was typical but didn't end normally. She and her husband started their Total Money Makeover at age twenty-five. They listened to me on our talk radio show and decided they'd had enough. They started with $20,000 in student loans, $10,000 in car loans, $3,000 in credit-card debt, and an $85,000 mortgage: a grand total of $118,000 in debt. On a $70,000 annual household income, they paid off every red cent in six years. At thirty-one years young, Al stood before me a smiling and free woman. She brought me one of my favorite gifts too. She brought me the letter and a Ziploc bag. What was in the bag? Fescue from her backyard, "Because," she said, "the grass really does feel different under my bare feet in the backyard now that there is no mortgage and we are DEBT-FREE!"

I asked what she was going to do now that she was debt-free. Her response was fun. She said she and her husband were going to dinner to celebrate. At dinner they were going to do two things. First, they were going to read the menu from left to right for a change, because money is now no object. Second, at the celebration dinner they fully intended to spend more than a car payment! You see, if you will live like no one else, later you can live like no one else.

Next, Al said she and her husband were on a direct course to the last Baby Step and would give more than they had ever imagined they would have. At thirty-one, this couple is destined for extreme levels of wealth. Congratulations, Al. You and your husband are true examples of what a Total Money Makeover looks like.

Don't have a mortgage yet? Scan the QR code below to use our mortgage calculator and find out how much home you can truly afford.

Already have a mortgage? Scan the QR code to learn how to pay it off early and become a debt-free homeowner.

12

Build Wealth Like Crazy: Become the Mr. Universe of Money

You have reached that perfect number, Baby Step Seven. By reaching the last step of your Total Money Makeover, you have entered the top 23 percent of Americans. You are totally debt-free—no house payment, no car payment. You are not Mastered by a Card, you have not Discovered bondage, American Excess has left your life, you have no student loans (your old pet), and you are free. You live on a monthly written plan and agree on it with your spouse, if you're married. You have a retirement destiny that looks considerably better than Alpo and Social Insecurity. If you have children, they will be students without student loans. You have lived like no one else, so now you will be able to live like no one else. Through sweat and sacrifice, you have reclaimed control of your life and your most powerful wealth-building tool, your income.

Baby Step Seven: Build Wealth and Give

What was the purpose of your having a Total Money Makeover? Why did you do it? Why all the sacrifice and work? To be in debt and out of control doesn't take nearly as much effort. Why go to all this trouble? Why do you want to have wealth? If you think wealth will answer all life's questions and make you trouble-free, you are delusional. I have had wealth twice in my life, and I don't find it to be trouble-free; as a matter of fact, most of the troubles have zeros on them. Wealth is not an escape mechanism. It is instead a tremendous responsibility. So what would you do if you had $18 million that it took you forty years to acquire?

After years of studying, teaching, and even preaching on this subject across America, I can find only three good uses for money. Money is good for FUN. Money is good to INVEST. And money is good to GIVE. Most anything else you find to do with it doesn't represent good mental and spiritual health on your part. So if you one day have $18 million, you should do all three of these things. In fact, while you are working the steps to wealth, you should be doing all three of these things. You have lost weight, you have built up your cardiovascular system, and now you have added muscle because you have lost the debt, saved for emergencies, and invested long term for retirement and college planning. At this stage in the Total Money Makeover, you are the Mr. Universe of Money, with serious abs, pecs, and quads. You have all this financial muscle, so now you should do something intentional with it. It is not just to look at. We built this financial superbody for a reason. To have FUN, INVEST, and GIVE.

Yes, We Get to Have Fun

The kid in us likes the FUN part of this equation, and since we have made this kid behave for a long time, with promises of ice cream if he does so, he should get some ice cream. Should anyone wear a $30,000 watch? Should anyone drive a brand-new $75,000 car? Should anyone live in a $1.5 million home? Absolutely, they should. The problem with people is, they buy those things when they can't afford them.

In chapter three on debt myths, we talked about new cars and what a bad investment they are. They go down in value very rapidly. Because the new car is the largest thing we buy that goes down in value, the car payment is usually our largest payment, except for the home mortgage. Roughly 70 percent of the people I assist in a Total Money Makeover have to make the difficult decision to sell their car so they can be free of the big payment. If they don't free themselves from this very large debt and very large payment, they find it very hard to climb the Baby Steps. So some days my talk radio show becomes the "sell the car" show. Some days it seems my answer to every question is, "Sell the car." "Don't buy that new car," is advice you will hear from me so often you'll be saying it in your sleep.

Sometimes a caller will ask if he can afford a purchase while on his Total Money Makeover. Sometimes a new listener wanders into the snare of asking about buying something totally ridiculous. I'm nice, at first, to explain that she can't do that now. I'll say something like, "The emergency fund is more important than a leather couch." I have a computer in front of me while I'm on the air, which the phone screener uses to tell me who is on hold and what they are calling about. Not long ago I looked down at the screen and saw that Michael was waiting to talk with me. The note said he wanted to buy a Harley-Davidson motorcycle. Harleys are fabulous bikes, but they are not for broke people, because a nice one will cost over $40,000. I prejudged Michael to be twenty-eight years old, with two car payments, two kids, one wife, and no money. I figured Michael was one of those guys who puts his little-boy fantasies before the good of his family. I loaded my gun to respond to his question. I was prepared not only to tell him not to buy a Harley but also to straighten out his whole way of looking at financial matters.

I figured Michael was probably making $48,000 per year and broke, so obviously he had no business buying a $40,000 toy. "Dave, I've always dreamed of owning a Harley," Michael started. "I just called to see if you thought I should buy one, and if I can afford it." For a few minutes I went on about how great Harleys are and how a lot of guys would love to have one. I usually ask a little about the caller's financial situation in order to make a quasi-reasonable judgment, so I asked Michael what he made last year. His response was, "$650,000." "Yeah, but what have you averaged over the last five years?" I asked, thinking he maybe hit the lotto. "About

$550,000 per year," was his answer. Now he had me on the ropes. "So how much do you have in investments?" I queried further. "About $20 million," came his final blow. "Buy the Harley, dude!" was my advice. Can Michael afford a $40,000 toy? Absolutely. Is it morally wrong for him to enjoy a fun item he wants when for him to purchase it as a percentage of his wealth is equal to most people buying a Happy Meal? No, there is absolutely nothing financially or morally wrong with that purchase. The man has earned his Harley and then some.

I told you Michael's story to make sure you understand that one reason to have a Total Money Makeover is to build wealth that allows you to have fun. So have some fun! Taking your family, even the extended ones, on a seven-day cruise, buying large diamonds, or even buying a new car are things you can afford to do when you have millions of dollars. You can afford to do these things because when you do them, your money position is hardly even affected. If you like travel, travel. If you like clothes, buy some. I am releasing you to have some fun with your money, because money is to be enjoyed. That guilt-free enjoyment is one of the three reasons to have a Total Money Makeover.

Investing Is How We Keep on Winning

The grown-up inside us likes the INVESTING of money because that is part of what makes you wealthy. Also, the growing dollars are a way of keeping score in our Total Money Makeover game. Are we winning? It truly becomes a game. In the movie *Two Weeks' Notice*, Hugh Grant plays George Ward. The character of George is a very wealthy and spoiled corporate figurehead. His character isn't one we want to imitate, but he has a great line in the movie about his wealth. He is telling Sandra Bullock's character that he lives in this luxury hotel, and he says nonchalantly, "Actually, I own the hotel; my life is a little bit like Monopoly."

Investing can feel like that after a while—"a little bit like Monopoly." When you are playing Monopoly, you can be up, or you can get behind.

Sometimes the market fluctuates, but as mature investors we ride out the waves and stay in for the long term. Sometimes I meet people who arrive at this step and are scared because just as they reach retirement age, their investments are heading down. Never fear; if you have quality investments with long-term track records, they will come back. Besides, you don't need all the nest egg at once to retire on; you just need some of the income from it. So since you don't need it all right then, it would be silly to cash everything out while the market is at the bottom. "Buy high; sell low" is not the formula to wealth. Be patient with the market while living off the income the nest egg produces.

You can choose to be a little more sophisticated, but until you have over $10 million, I would keep your investing very simple. You can clutter your life with a bunch of unnecessary stress by getting into extremely complex investments. I use simple mutual funds and debt-free real estate as my investment mix—very clean, simple investments with some basic tax advantages. As you arrive at this Baby Step, if you want to own some paid-for real estate, it can be fun.

Always manage your own money. You should surround yourself with a team of people smarter than you, but you make the decisions. You can tell if they are smarter than you if they can explain complex issues in ways you can understand. If a member of your team wants you to do something "because I say so," get a new team member. You are not hiring a daddy; you are gathering counsel. God did not give them the responsibility over this money. He gave that to you. Celebrities and pro athletes often lose their entire fortunes because they give up the responsibility of managing their own money. The money manager who loses your hard-earned investments won't live with the regret and pain that you will. The Bible states, "In the multitude of counselors there is safety" (Prov. 11:14 NKJV). A good estate-planning attorney, a CPA or tax expert, an insurance pro, an investment pro, and a good real estate agent are a few of the essential team members you should gather around you. I endorse the use of financial planners if they are team members and not the sole captains of their teams.

When selecting and working with your wealth team, it is vital to bring on only members who have the heart of a teacher, not the heart of a salesman or the heart of an "expert." The salesman is always chasing a commission and thinking short term, and the "expert" can't help being condescending, which is humorous because they likely have less money than you. Also, when taking advice, evaluate if the person giving the advice will profit from the advice. If your insurance pro is coming up with more great insurance ideas every week, you may have a problem. That is not to say everyone who makes a commission off you is out to get you. There are plenty of commission-only financial people who have extreme levels of integrity. Just be aware of possible conflicts of interest. To find investment advisors who serve your area, scan the QR code below. You can even find tax, insurance, and real estate pros as well as other providers.

Everyone knows that the pay for a schoolteacher isn't great. With an income of less than $40,000, one adopted son, and no plans for our financial future, I knew we had to make some changes. We heard about Dave Ramsey's plan at our church, and we were so inspired that we set a goal to pay off our $50,000 mortgage in five years. We knew that to have a Total Money Makeover, vacations and fancy toys were out, and we would have to tighten our budget considerably. But we were excited about what was at the finish line.

I started a few side businesses—tax prep and eBay—and was able to add about $15,000 extra income to our payment. With all of this extra income, you might think that paying off a $50,000 mortgage would be easy to do in five years, but our plans to adopt a little girl from China were priority. The adoption costs were around $17,000, and just when we didn't think we would be able to get pregnant . . . surprise! Our health insurance did not cover childbirth, so we had an additional $5,000 added to our payments.

With a growing family, we were more determined than ever to get rid of the house payment. And praise the Lord! We did it in just less than four years! We beat our goal by a full year. That just proves if we can do this, anyone can.

Now that we are on the other side, it is so awesome. It is such a peaceful feeling to know that money does not control us. Even though I am still a teacher, and my wife stays home with our kids . . . NOW we can take those vacations and buy fancy toys. PLUS, we've adopted another girl from China, making us a family of five on a teacher's salary. We're able to give freely to people and organizations we believe in that focus on orphaned children in China.

We give like never before; we save like never before; and, most important, we live life the way God intended us to like never before.

Keith (age 40) and
Karen (age 42) McGinty
Math Teacher; Stay-at-Home Mom

Within Baby Step Seven (Build Wealth and Give), there is a subsection b, another milestone. The second milestone within becoming wealthy is the "Pinnacle Point."

Growing up in the suburbs in Tennessee, I grew accustomed to riding a bike and facing hills. To a seven-year-old with one gear, a huge hill looked like Mount Everest. I don't know which kid in history did it first, but the technique for small-guy bike hill climbing has been passed down for generations—the switchback. Instead of pedaling straight up, we would painfully go side to side, taking a small bite at a time of our Tennessee mountain. The unpopular players' baseball cards made a slow *click, click, click* through the spokes as we made our ascent. The heat seemed oven-like, and the beads of sweat turned to rivers. This is the time a seven-year-old pushes with every muscle in his being. The strain and determination show on your face like last year's Halloween mask. You pull on the handlebars with all the power your arm muscles will produce to push your legs down on the pedals one more time. Push, push, breathe, breathe—until you finally reach the top.

What do you find at the top? The cynical among us just said, "Another hill to climb." Those of us with a kid still alive inside know what was at the top. Those of us who still have a kid inside who can dream, who can believe, and who can hope know what we found at the top. Those of us who have pushed up some unbelievable hills know what I found that Tennessee summer day at the top of the hill. I found that perfect moment. The perfect moment when you push the pedal the last time before going down a huge hill on the other side. The perfect moment when you hang in the balance, after all the sweat, the work, and the agony, and a smile breaks across your face. That moment just before you take the glorious ride down is the Pinnacle Point.

And the ride down *is* glorious. The wind blows through your hair, and your feet are not on the pedals anymore but on the handlebars. The *click, click, click* of the baseball cards becomes a chattering with a sound like thousands of crickets. You are now enjoying the ride; the coasting is the fruit of your labors. Memories of strain, sweat, and repeated near failure fade as the sun shines and the wind tickles your ears, whispering, "You are the king! You did it! You climbed the hill! You didn't quit! You paid the price to win!" The smile in your soul says, "*Accomplishment.*"

If you are beginning to think I'm being a little overdramatic, so be it. It is hard to describe reaching the Pinnacle Point without some emotion. This Baby Step takes us to the point at which your money works harder than you do, the Pinnacle Point. It is the instant in time where focused gazelle intensity has reached critical mass, and your money takes on a life of its own.

This point is not that you are going to quit life when you get there; you will still manage and direct, but the money thing will have its feet up, and you will be coasting downhill. Wealth will find its way to you. Mistakes on your tax return will be in your favor; the IRS will discover them and send you the money back with interest. Well, that's probably an impossible dream, but you get the idea.

When your money makes more than you do, you are officially wealthy. When you can comfortably live on your investment income, you are financially secure. Money is a hard worker, harder than you. Money never gets sick, never gets pregnant, and is never disabled. Money works twenty-four hours a day, seven days a week. Money gets its job done, and it asks only for directions and a firm master.

You have reached the Pinnacle Point when you can live off 8 percent of your nest egg. Go ahead, multiply your nest egg by .08, and if you can live on that number or that number is more than you make, you are coasting downhill. Congratulations! Your money makes more than you do! By doing this calculation, you will discover how close you are to hitting this major financial security milestone. You will be able to calculate what your Pinnacle Point nest egg is, and then, using all your available income, see how many years it will take you to climb that hill. Believe me, everything is downhill after that. Enjoy the ride.

Giving Is the Biggest Reward of the Entire Workout

The most mature part of who you are will meet the kid inside as you learn to involve yourself in the last use of money, which is to GIVE it away. Giving is possibly the most fun you will ever have with money. FUN is good, but you will tire of golf and travel, and if you eat it enough, lobster starts tasting like soap. INVESTING is good, but going around and around that Monopoly board eventually loses its appeal—especially after you reach the Pinnacle Point. Every mentally and spiritually healthy person I've met has been turned on by giving as long as it didn't mean his own lights got cut off. I can promise you from meeting with literally thousands of millionaires that the thing the healthy ones share in common is a love of GIVING.

Only the strong can help the weak, and that is true of money too. A toddler is not allowed to carry a newborn; only adults who have the muscular strength to ensure safety should carry babies. If you want to help someone, many times you can't do so without money. The Bible states that pure religion is actually helping the poor, not theorizing over why they are poor (see James 1:27). Margaret Thatcher said, "No one would remember the Good Samaritan if he'd only had good intentions; he had money as well." The Good Samaritan had a good heart and a heavy enough purse to pay an innkeeper to help take care of the injured man. Money was involved. Money was at its best that day. Money gives power to good intentions. That's why I'm unashamedly in favor of building wealth.

My father died when I was five years old, so it was just me, my two sisters, and my mom for most of my life. She did the best she could, but I never really had anyone to talk to about financial issues. So I ended up going deeply into debt buying a lot of stupid things.

After getting married and having a daughter, my wife and I decided that we needed to get out of debt and start saving for the future. It took a while for us to get on a plan because we were each going our own way with our money. But eventually we decided to get rid of our debt once and for all!

We've paid off $50,000, and with no new credit activity, our FICO score has taken a hit. But we don't care—we don't worship the almighty credit score anymore! We cut up all our credit cards, put $10,000 into our emergency fund, and we're now debt-free except for the house!

Now that we're doing well financially, we have money to give when we feel called to. Last year our daughter's friend lost her father right before school started. Her mother was on temporary disability with little income coming in, which made her private school tuition a huge burden. Because I knew the pain of losing a parent, I didn't want our daughter's friend to deal with the loss of her father and the trauma of changing schools. So my wife and I decided to step up and help by paying the girl's school tuition for the year. She was able to stay with her friends during that hard time in her life, and we were blessed to be able to help!

Buying things may feel good, but giving always feels right. We're thankful that God has taught us how to handle our money because now we can look for ways to bless others financially. All the "stuff" in the world can't compare to the feeling of helping others in need.

Ron (age 44) and
Teresa (age 46) Brewer
Sales; Staff Children's Clinic

Let Go

Sadly, I meet people who try to avoid this third use of money, mistakenly thinking they will end up with more. Eric Butterworth tells of an interesting system used to capture monkeys in the jungle. The captors use heavy glass bottles with long necks. Into each bottle they deposit some sweet-smelling nuts. The aroma of the nuts attracts a monkey to the bottle. When the monkey puts its hand into the bottle to get the nuts, the neck of the bottle is too small for its fist to come back out. The monkey can't take his hand out of the bottle without dropping the nuts, which he is unwilling to do. The bottles are too heavy to carry away, so the monkey becomes trapped by nothing more than greed. We may smile at these foolish monkeys, but how many times has our freedom been taken away by nothing more than our greed?

Most of us have given something at some time or another, but I have seen some really fun things happen when good people become wealthy. When you have your Total Money Makeover, you can do some things with scale. I have one friend who buys seventy-five brand-new bikes for an inner-city ministry every year. He gets these bikes at Christmas and, in conjunction with a missionary group that knows the families in the area, gives them out one at a time to kids in a subsidized housing project. The project is drug-infested and crime-riddled, but for one day a year, those young people see someone who wants nothing in return.

Another pastor friend of mine is involved in a project called Seeds of Kindness. An anonymous member of his congregation gave $50,000 to the congregation members to give away, one $100 bill at a time. The member must not use the gift, the member must receive nothing in return, and it should be given as personally as possible. These $100 bills are given human to human across the city with fabulous results. People who had completely lost faith in God and in the human race are shaken to the core by a simple $100 gift. The givers often report having more fun than the receivers.

Secret Santa

We all have seen these powerful examples of giving. *USA Today* followed a guy who called himself Secret Santa at Christmas for several years. Secret Santa walked the streets around Christmastime and gave away $100 bills. Nothing required, nothing expected. Sometimes he gave to people in need, and other times he just gave. Every year he gave away around $25,000 in $100 bills. He started this tradition years ago in his hometown of Kansas City and moved out across America. He gave in New York after 9/11 and in the Virginia/Washington, D.C., area after the sniper attacks. He just walked around and handed people $100 bills. He got some fabulous reactions and heard some wonderful stories.

In late winter of 1971, he worked as a salesman, and when his company went broke, Santa found himself broke too. He had slept in his car for eight days and hadn't eaten for two days when he went to the Dixie Diner. He ordered and ate a big breakfast. He waited for the crowd to clear, then acted as if he had lost his wallet. The diner's owner, Tom Horn, who was also the cook, came over near the stool where Santa had been sitting, picked up a $20 bill, and said, "Son, you must have dropped this." Santa realized later that Tom had planted that twenty to let him out of a sticky situation with his dignity intact. As he drove away, Santa said, "Thank You, Lord, for that man, and I promise if I ever have money, I will do the same."

In 1999, Santa, now a very successful businessman, looked up Tom Horn, now eighty-five years old, in his home of Tupelo, Mississippi. Santa recounted the story of the hungry young man of 1971 while standing on Tom's porch in a Santa hat. He asked Tom what he thought that $20 would be worth by that time, and Tom laughingly said, "Probably $10,000." Santa then handed Tom $10,000 cash in an envelope. Of course, Tom tried to hand it back, but finally Santa won out, so Tom deposited the money in the bank. He said he might need it to take care of his wife, who had Alzheimer's.

Horn said of Secret Santa, "He doesn't want any thanks or praise for what he does. He does it out of the goodness of his heart." After giving to dozens of people a few Christmases ago, Santa said, "Isn't it fun to lift people up and see the smiles on their faces?" I think I know why this Santa gave. He gave because it is the most fun he can possibly have with money, and you will never know until you try.

A few years ago Secret Santa's identity was revealed. He was Larry Stewart from Kansas City. Larry revealed his identity because, after giving away over $1.3 million, he had been diagnosed with cancer. Larry's wish was that we all continue his legacy of being Secret Santas. Talk about paying it forward!

Do All Three

There are only three uses for money: FUN, INVESTING, and GIVING. You cannot claim Total Money Makeover status until you do all three. You don't have to buy a Harley, invest millions, or give away $25,000 cash, but you do have to do some of each. And as I said earlier, you should begin doing some of each as you go through the steps. Giving something, even if it is just giving your time by serving soup to the homeless, should start from Baby Step One. Fun also begins there, although it has to be inexpensive fun in the beginning; the fun gets bigger and better as we get higher in the steps. Investing, of course, begins at Baby Step Four (Invest 15 Percent of Your Income in Retirement). You are not getting the full use and enjoyment of your money unless you do all three.

Someone who never has fun with money misses the point. Someone who never invests money will never have any. Someone who never gives is a monkey with his hand in a bottle. Do some of each, and if you are married, let your spouse have some slack as soon as there is some. After you get past the emergency-fund step, let each other function in the areas you like best. My wife, Sharon, is a natural saver, so she always cheats toward investing. I am a natural spender, so I make sure she has fun. We both enjoy giving.

Please push that pedal one more time. Switchback if you have to; failure is not an option. Push, push! I promise, and the tens of thousands who have reached their Pinnacle Point in their Total Money Makeover promise, at the top of the hill is a glorious ride down. Take that ride with us!

Scan the QR code below to learn more about expanding your investing in Baby Step Seven.

I was weird before weird was cool. I started saving for my first home at age seventeen and paid half down at age twenty-three. My wife, on the other hand, was slightly different. When we got married, she had thirteen credit cards and a car payment totaling $30,000. I knew this was not a good place to be as newlyweds, so we agreed to become debt-free.

Even though my wife was a little reluctant, we started to work on paying off the consumer debt and the $95,000 on our new house. This is when I found out about the Total Money Makeover and decided to get intense. So I started a part-time lawn-care business using the tools I already had, and my mother-in-law let me use her riding mower as long as I cut her yard every Saturday. We started paying off bills left and right.

My wife dreamed about being a stay-at-home mom for our kids. So with the help of the booming lawn-care business and a tight budget, we killed the consumer debt in ten months, and when we decided to start a family, she was able to do just that. For a long time, we put almost every free cent toward paying off our mortgage, and today we can proudly scream, "We're debt-free!"

Arguments about money are gone. If something breaks, we just fix it or replace it. It's not even a concern. I have all the time I want to spend with my family knowing that their future is going to be bright because we sacrificed for it.

A short time after paying off the house, we started Baby Step Seven, and let me tell you . . . giving money away is a great feeling, and it's easy to do when you are debt-free. Our traditional and Roth IRAs are funded, as well as college funds for our two boys. Investing is key! You have to do it NOW because you can't get that time back. Later in life, you will be so happy you did. Now we can retire the way we want to and when we want to. Today we have over $100,000 in retirement funds, $90,000 in savings, our house is now worth $450,000, and we've paid cash for two newer cars. So my status symbol of choice is the paid-off home mortgage AND the BMW in the driveway.

Luke (age 36) and
Laura (age 34) Lokietek
Senior Programmer Analyst;
Homemaker

13

Live Like No One Else

You started this book financially flabby, overweight with debt, out of shape in savings, and in desperate need of a personal trainer. In these pages, you have reviewed how tens of thousands of ordinary people have gotten into great financial shape. This is a book about getting out of debt and into wealth. However, there is a problem with following the Total Money Makeover plan. The problem is simply that it's a "proven plan" because it works. If you follow this system, it *will* work. It will work so well that you are going to become wealthy over the next twenty to forty years. The problem with becoming wealthy is that you stand a chance of becoming enamored with wealth. We can easily start to worship money, especially after we have some.

False Cents of Security

According to Proverbs 10:15, a rich man's wealth can become his walled city. In Bible times, the wall around the city was the city's protection from the enemy. If all you get from your wealth is the wrong view of it, wealth will destroy your peace. If you get from your wealth the idea that you are some big deal because you gathered some money, you missed the essence of a Total Money Makeover. The wealthy person who is ruled by his stuff is no freer than the debt-ridden consumer we have picked on throughout the book. Antoine Rivaroli said, "There are men who gain from their wealth only the fear of losing it."

Since you have read many pages learning a wealth-building system from me, you might think that I believe stuff is the answer to happiness, emotional well-being, and spiritual maturity. You would be wrong because I know that is not the case. On the contrary, I see a real spiritual danger to having great wealth. The danger is old-fashioned materialism. In his great book *Money, Possessions, and Eternity*, author Randy Alcorn takes a probing look at materialism. Randy discusses a disease running amuck in America: "affluenza." Affluenza is a malady that affects some of the affluent and their children. Because some of the affluent and their children seek happiness, solace, and fulfillment in the consuming of stuff, they face a problem. By trying to get stuff to do something it wasn't designed to do, they come up empty and end up depressed and even suicidal. They discover bumper-sticker wisdom: "He who dies with the most toys is still dead." Stuff is wonderful; get some stuff, but don't let the pursuit of wealth become your god.

My wife and I were concerned that our wealth could be a curse and not a blessing to our children. So we were tough on our kids when they were young regarding work, saving, giving, and spending issues. From the time they were little, we expected a lot from them. Today, I am very proud of the character of our adult children. They, like their parents, aren't perfect, but they are doing well. When one of my kids was a teenager, she complained to me, "Do you know how tough it is being Dave Ramsey's kid? Dad, you are so hard on us, making us buy our own cars, manage our own checkbooks. You cut us no slack." I replied that we are tough on them because one day they will inherit our wealth, and that wealth will either ruin their lives or become a tool for great good.

My kids, you, and I can have good things happen as a result of our Total Money Makeover only *if* we have the spiritual character to recognize that wealth is not the answer to life's questions. We further must recognize that while wealth is very fun, it comes with great responsibility.

Another paradox is that wealth will make you more of what you are. Let that one soak in for a minute. If you are a jerk and you become wealthy, you will be king of the jerks. If you are generous and you become wealthy, you will be most generous. If you are kind, wealth will allow you to show kindness in immeasurable ways. If you feel guilty, wealth will ensure that you feel guilty for the rest of your life.

The LOVE of Money, Not Money, Is the Root of All Kinds of Evil

As a Christian, I am amazed how certain political and religious groups have decided that wealth is evil. Many of the heroes of biblical faith, of world history, and of our nation were very wealthy, including King David, Solomon, Job, and most of our Founding Fathers. There is a negative mindset justifying money mediocrity that is maddening. Wealth is not evil, and people who possess it aren't evil by virtue of the wealth. There are rich jerks and poor jerks. Dallas Willard, in his book *The Spirit of the Disciplines*, says to *use* riches is to cause them to be consumed, to *trust* in riches is to count upon them for things they cannot provide, but to *possess* riches is to have the right to say how they will or will not be used.

If you are a good person, it is your spiritual duty to possess riches for the good of mankind. If you are a Christian like me, it is your spiritual duty to possess riches so that you can do with them things that bring glory to God. The bottom line is, if you take the stand that managing wealth is evil or carnal, then by default you leave all the wealth to the evil, carnal people. If wealth is spiritually bad, then good people can't have it, so all the bad people get it. It is the duty of the good people to get wealth to keep it from the bad people because the good people will do good with it. If we all abandon money because some misguided souls view it as evil, then the only ones with money will be the pornographer, the drug dealer, or the pimp. Simple enough?

To Give You Hope

I think you can tell by now that the Total Money Makeover is more than just a discussion on money issues. The Total Money Makeover makes you face the man or woman in the mirror. Facing that man or woman makes us face emotional, relational, physical, and even spiritual aspects of our lives. The wealthy people that I know who are fulfilled didn't just have a Total *MONEY* Makeover. They had a life makeover. Because personal finance is 80 percent behavior and 20 percent knowledge, you will either make your life over in this process, or you will end up miserable. I'm being very spiritual here at the end, but the spiritual is a legitimate aspect of behavior. I see well-rounded, mature people who become all God designed them to be when they get their money closets cleaned out. God has a plan for your life, and that plan isn't to harm you; it is a plan for your future to give you hope (see Jeremiah 29:11).

Hope is what I want you to walk away with from this book. Hope that you can be like the people whose stories I told in this book. Hope that you can turn your money troubles into money triumphs. Hope that you can retire with dignity. Hope that you can change your family tree, because by building wealth you leave an inheritance. Hope that you can give money in a way you have never given before. It is time for you to become a gazelle. It is time for you to leave the reading and the classroom behind and apply these principles. They are age-old principles, and they work. Tens of thousands of ordinary people just like you and me have become debt-free and even wealthy using this plan. It isn't magic; it is common sense. The exciting thing is, anyone can do this—*anyone*. Are you next? I hope so.

Start Your Total Money Makeover Here

We have a tradition on *The Ramsey Show*. It began by accident long ago when a listener called in and immediately began screaming at me that she was debt-free. I couldn't even get a word in edgewise! She'd felt trapped by her debt for so long that once she finally broke free, all she wanted to do was shout about her victory at the top of her lungs! Today, Debt-Free Screams are a regular part of our show. Many times, folks come in person to do their scream from the Debt-Free Stage in the lobby of our headquarters and share the stories of their debt-free journeys. It is both a victory dance for them and encouragement for all those who are still on their journey. I always ask them what made the biggest difference as they worked the Baby Steps. What made them succeed where others do not? The answer? Time and again, it's two simple words: the budget. Whether they paid off $10,000 in debt or $500,000; had an income of $30,000 or $230,000; were married or single; old or young, learning to live on a budget is always the primary factor in their success.

People who have never budgeted often have strong feelings about the idea of budgeting. A lot of you believe a budget is restrictive and if you live on one, you'll never be able to spend money on anything fun again. But I'll tell you something that's truly not fun: feeling that you're out of control with your money, that you're barely getting by, or that you will never get ahead.

Budgeting will change all of that for you because at its core, a budget is just a plan for your money. It's how you tell your money where to go so you can stop wondering where it went. When you budget, you'll know the basics (food, shelter, utilities, transportation) are covered. No more anxiety about the debit card getting declined at the grocery store—or worse, putting the groceries on a credit card. No more late notices for the mortgage payment. When you use your budget to pay extra on your debt, guess what? Your debt gets paid off! When you budget money to save for your emergency fund, or Christmas, or a new car, guess what? You actually save money for those goals! Good budgeting is so pivotal to your success with the Baby Steps that we think of it as Baby Step 0, and it's the step you never stop.

If you're married, budgeting together will help you get on the same page with your spouse about money and finally put an end to those money fights. You'll be on the same team, working toward the same goals. Can you imagine the peace that will bring to your home? If you're single, but don't budget, you already know how easy it is to hide your spending, even from yourself. That's why you've got to budget too—to be accountable to yourself and the goals you set.

For your Total Money Makeover to succeed, you've got to plan your spending every month, on paper, on purpose, before the month begins. I say "on paper" because that's the way Sharon and I started our budgeting—on a yellow legal notepad. But you don't have to be as old school (or nerdy) as I was because my team has created, hands down, the best budgeting app in the world. It's called EveryDollar and millions of people use it every day to build their budgets, track their spending, and make real progress on their money goals. We believe so strongly in the importance of a budget for your success that we're giving you access to the premium version of EveryDollar for three months—totally free! With the premium version, you can connect your bank accounts and stream your transactions right into your budget. Plus, you'll get access to all sorts of resources to help you build your budgeting skills and reports to keep you on track. And the team is adding new features all the time!

I won't promise you will love budgeting after the first month. It takes about three months to really start to get the hang of it. So don't give up. What I will promise is if you keep working at and stick to the budget you create, you will start to see progress. You will finally feel in control of your money. You and your spouse will have better communication about money. You will have hope that your Total Money Makeover is going to work. All you have to do is scan the QR code below and get started!

About the Author

America's trusted voice on money and business, Dave Ramsey is a personal money-management expert and extremely popular national radio personality. He's authored five *New York Times* best-selling books: *Financial Peace*, *More Than Enough*, *The Total Money Makeover*, *EntreLeadership*, and *Baby Steps Millionaires*. *The Ramsey Show* is heard by millions of listeners each week on hundreds of radio stations throughout the United States. Dave is the founder and CEO of Ramsey Solutions—a company dedicated to helping people achieve financial freedom, set career goals, and strengthen relationships through *Financial Peace University* classes, personal finance curriculum, world-class Live Events, informative podcasts, and more.

Total Money Makeover Worksheets

For the digital version of these worksheets,
visit ramseysolutions.com/tools. And check out the
EveryDollar app at Ramseysolutions.com/budgeting.

Monthly Cash Flow Plan

Yes, this budget form has a lot of lines and blanks.

But that's okay. We do that so we can list practically every expense imaginable on this form to prevent you from forgetting something. Don't expect to put something on every line. Just use the ones that are relevant to your specific situation.

Step 1

Enter your monthly take-home pay in the box at the top right (**A**). This is the amount you have for the month to budget. So far so good, huh?

Step 2

Within each main category, such as Food, there are subcategories, like Groceries. Start at the top and work your way down, filling out the Budgeted column (**B**) first. Add up each subcategory and put that number in the Total box (**C**).

Also, pay attention to Dave's recommended percentages (**D**). This will help you keep from budgeting too much for a category.

Step 3

Finally, enter your take-home pay in the top box at the end of the page (**E**), then add up all categories and place that total in the Category Totals box (**F**). Then subtract your Category Totals amount from your Take-Home Pay. You should have a zero balance (**G**). Doesn't that feel great?

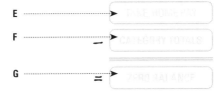

Step 4

When the month ends, put what you actually spent in the Spent column (**H**). That will help you make any necessary adjustments to the next month's budget.

Monthly Cash Flow Plan

Monthly Take-Home Pay [ ]

Add up budgeted column & enter here

These icons represent good options for cash envelopes

❤ CHARITY
	Spent	Budgeted
Tithes		
Charity & Offerings		
*10–15%		TOTAL

🐷 SAVING
	Spent	Budgeted
Emergency Fund		
Retirement Fund		
College Fund		
*10–15%		TOTAL

🏠 HOUSING
	Spent	Budgeted
First Mortgage/Rent		
Second Mortgage		
Real Estate Taxes		
Repairs/Maint.		
Association Dues		
*25–35%		TOTAL

⚙ UTILITIES
	Spent	Budgeted
Electricity		
Gas		
Water		
Trash		
Phone/Mobile		
Internet		
Cable		
*5–10%		TOTAL

🍎 FOOD
	Spent	Budgeted
Groceries		
Restaurants		
*5–15%		TOTAL

👕 CLOTHING
	Spent	Budgeted
Adults		
Children		
Cleaning/Laundry		
*2–7%		TOTAL

🚗 TRANSPORTATION
	Spent	Budgeted
Gas & Oil		
Repairs & Tires		
License & Taxes		
Car Replacement		
Other _____		
*10–15%		TOTAL

🩺 MEDICAL/HEALTH
	Spent	Budgeted
Medications		
Doctor Bills		
Dentist		
Optometrist		
Vitamins		
Other _____		
Other _____		
*5–10%		TOTAL

*Dave's Recommended Percentages

🛡 INSURANCE

	Spent	Budgeted
Life Insurance		
Health Insurance		
Homeowner/Renter		
Auto Insurance		
Disability Insurance		
Identity Theft		
Long-Term Care		
*10–25%		TOTAL

👤 PERSONAL

	Spent	Budgeted
Child Care/Sitter		
Toiletries		
Cosmetics/Hair Care		
Education/Tuition		
Books/Supplies		
Child Support		
Alimony		
Subscriptions		
Organization Dues		
Gifts (incl. Christmas)		
Replace Furniture		
Pocket Money (His)		
Pocket Money (Hers)		
Baby Supplies		
Pet Supplies		
Music/Technology		
Miscellaneous		
Other _____		
Other _____		
Other _____		
*5–10%		TOTAL

🏃 RECREATION

	Spent	Budgeted
Entertainment		
Vacation		
*5–10%		TOTAL

🔑 DEBTS

	Spent	Budgeted
Car Payment 1		
Car Payment 2		
Credit Card 1 _____		
Credit Card 2 _____		
Credit Card 3 _____		
Credit Card 4 _____		
Credit Card 5 _____		
Student Loan 1		
Student Loan 2		
Student Loan 3		
Student Loan 4		
Other _____		
Other _____		
Other _____		
Other _____		
Other _____		

Your goal is 0% → | *5–10% | | TOTAL |

Once you have completed filling out each category, subtract all category totals from your take-home pay.

Use the "income sources" form if necessary → [TAKE-HOME PAY]

Add up totals from each category − [CATEGORY TOTALS]

Remember— The goal of a zero-based budget is to get this number to zero = [ZERO BALANCE]

Allocated Spending Plan

Life pulls your money in all directions. Spend time here before spending your cash.

Allocation is a fancy word for "when you spend your money." We're going to build on your Monthly Cash Flow Plan here and get a little more in depth by breaking your income down by pay period. The four columns on this form represent the four weeks in a given month. If you're married, combine your spouse's income with yours.

Step 1a

Fill out the pay period in box A. This is simply how long you'll go between paychecks. If you get paid on the 1st and 15th, then your pay period for July, for example, would be 7/1 to 7/14.

A ---------------------------------

Pay Period Dates	
Pay Period Income	

B ---------------------------------

Step 1b

Write how much you will be paid in that pay period (B).

Step 2

Write down how much money you're budgeting in the Budgeted column (C). In the Remaining column (D), keep a running total of how much of your starting income you have left for that pay period.

C

D

🏠 HOUSING	Budgeted	Remaining
First Mortgage/Rent	945	285
Second Mortgage		
Real Estate Taxes	150	135

Step 3

Keep going down the list until the Remaining column (E) hits zero. When Remaining equals zero, you're done budgeting for that pay period.

E

Optometrist	40	95
Vitamins	20	75
Other _____		

Step 4

If you have money left over at the end of the column (F), go back and adjust an area, such as Savings or Giving, so that you spend every single dollar. Every dollar needs a home.

F

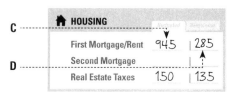

Other Final cable bill	40	35
Other Florist bill	35	0
Other _____		

Allocated Spending Plan

Pay Period Dates

Pay Period Income

Income
− Tithes
= Remaining to budget this pay period

♥ CHARITY

	Budgeted	Remaining	Budgeted	Remaining	Budgeted	Remaining	Budgeted	Remaining
Tithes								
Charity & Offerings								

"Remaining" minus "Budgeted." Back & forth.

🐷 SAVING

	Budgeted	Remaining	Budgeted	Remaining	Budgeted	Remaining	Budgeted	Remaining
Emergency Fund								
Retirement Fund								
College Fund								
Other _____								
Other _____								

🏠 HOUSING

	Budgeted	Remaining	Budgeted	Remaining	Budgeted	Remaining	Budgeted	Remaining
First Mortgage/Rent								
Second Mortgage								
Real Estate Taxes								
Repairs/Maint.								
Association Dues								
Other _____								
Other _____								

⚙ UTILITIES

	Budgeted	Remaining	Budgeted	Remaining	Budgeted	Remaining	Budgeted	Remaining
Electricity								
Gas								
Water								
Trash								
Phone/Mobile								
Internet								
Cable								
Other _____								
Other _____								

Pay Period Dates

When "Remaining" equals zero, you're done budgeting for this pay period.

🍎 FOOD

	Budgeted	Remaining	Budgeted	Remaining	Budgeted	Remaining	Budgeted	Remaining
Groceries								
Restaurants								

👕 CLOTHING

	Budgeted	Remaining	Budgeted	Remaining	Budgeted	Remaining	Budgeted	Remaining
Adults								
Children								
Cleaning/Laundry								

🚗 TRANSPORTATION

	Budgeted	Remaining	Budgeted	Remaining	Budgeted	Remaining	Budgeted	Remaining
Gas & Oil								
Repairs & Tires								
License & Taxes								
Car Replacement								
Other								
Other								
Other								

🩺 MEDICAL/HEALTH

	Budgeted	Remaining	Budgeted	Remaining	Budgeted	Remaining	Budgeted	Remaining
Medications								
Doctor Bills								
Dentist								
Optometrist								
Vitamins								
Other								
Other								
Other								
Other								
Other								
Other								

Allocated Spending Plan

Pay Period Dates				
Pay Period Income				

🛡 INSURANCE

	Budgeted	Remaining	Budgeted	Remaining	Budgeted	Remaining	Budgeted	Remaining
Life Insurance								
Health Insurance								
Homeowner/Renter								
Auto Insurance								
Disability Insurance								
Identity Theft								
Long-Term Care								

👤 PERSONAL

	Budgeted	Remaining	Budgeted	Remaining	Budgeted	Remaining	Budgeted	Remaining
Child Care/Sitter								
Toiletries								
Cosmetics								
Education/Tuition								
Books/Supplies								
Child Support								
Alimony								
Subscriptions								
Org. Dues								
Gifts (incl. Christmas)								
Replace Furniture								
Pocket Money (His)								
Pocket Money (Hers)								
Baby Supplies								
Pet Supplies								
Music/Technology								
Miscellaneous								
Other _____								
Other _____								
Other _____								

| Pay Period Dates | TO | TO | TO | TO |

🏃 RECREATION	Budgeted	Remaining	Budgeted	Remaining	Budgeted	Remaining	Budgeted	Remaining
✉ Entertainment								
Vacation								
Other _____								

🔑 DEBTS	Budgeted	Remaining	Budgeted	Remaining	Budgeted	Remaining	Budgeted	Remaining
Car Payment 1								
Car Payment 2								
Credit Card 1 _____								
Credit Card 2 _____								
Credit Card 3 _____								
Credit Card 4 _____								
Credit Card 5 _____								
Student Loan 1								
Student Loan 2								
Student Loan 3								
Student Loan 4								
Other _____								
Other _____								
Other _____								
Other _____								
Other _____								
Other _____								
Other _____								
Other _____								
Other _____								
Other _____								
Other _____								
Other _____								
Other _____								

Irregular Income Planning

Some people's paychecks all look the same, and some people's don't.

If you're self-employed or in sales, you really understand this! But you're not free from filling out budgets. As a matter of fact, this form is vital for just that reason! It can be easy for debts and expenses to overtake what you're bringing in. Stay on top of your money here.

Step 1

Fill in the Monthly Cash Flow Plan form based on what you reasonably expect to bring home for the month. If you aren't sure, use last year's lowest income month as your starting point.

Step 2

List anything that didn't make it in your Monthly Cash Flow Plan in the Items column (**A**). These are the things that you couldn't budget for but need to be funded.

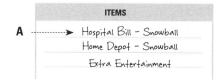

ITEMS
Hospital Bill – Snowball
Home Depot – Snowball
Extra Entertainment

A

Step 3

Rewrite your expenses in priority order and keep a running total. Setting good priorities is crucial here. For instance, a beach trip is not more important than putting food on the table!

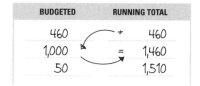

BUDGETED	RUNNING TOTAL
460	+ 460
1,000	= 1,460
50	1,510

Step 4

When you get paid, write any additional income in the box (**B**). *Additional* means anything above and beyond what you budgeted on the Monthly Cash Flow Plan form.

B

Additional Irregular Income 1,500

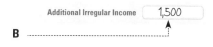

Step 5

Spend your money right down the list until it's all gone. You most likely won't make it all the way down the list. That's okay! That's why it's important to prioritize.

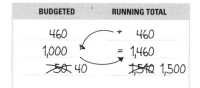

BUDGETED	RUNNING TOTAL
460	+ 460
1,000	= 1,460
~~50~~ 40	~~1,510~~ 1,500

Irregular Income Planning

Any additional irregular income goes here

Additional Irregular Income [　　　　　　]

List, in priority order, anything that didn't make it in your monthly cash flow plan

Work back & forth, adding each budgeted item to the running total

ITEMS	BUDGETED	RUNNING TOTAL
		+
		=

Debt Snowball

You've got your emergency fund taken care of. Now it's time to dump the debt!

The Debt Snowball form will help you get some quick wins and develop some serious momentum! You'll make minimum payments on all of your debts except for the smallest one. Then attack that one with gazelle intensity! Throw every dollar at it that you can!

Step 1

List your debts in order from the smallest Total Payoff balance to the largest. Don't be concerned with interest rates unless two debts have a similar payoff balance. In that case, list the one with the higher interest rate first.

DEBTS	TOTAL PAYOFF
Diagnostic	50
Hospital Bill	460
Home Depot	770

Step 2

Attack that smallest debt by paying as much on it as you possibly can. Once you pay off one debt, take what you *were* paying on that one and add it to the minimum payment of the *next* debt. As the snowball rolls over, it picks up more snow. Get it?

MIN. PAYMENT	NEW PAYMENT
~~10~~	~~10~~
~~38~~	~~48~~
45	93

Step 3

Every time you pay off a debt, cross the debt off. This will show you how close you're getting to becoming debt-free!

~~Hospital Bill~~
~~Home Depot~~
~~Chase VISA~~
~~Car Loan~~   I'M DEBT-FREE!!!!!

Debt Snowball

Once a debt is paid off, add the next minimum payment to your current amount. This becomes the new payment.

List your debts smallest to largest by <u>balance</u>

DEBTS	TOTAL PAYOFF	MIN. PAYMENT	NEW PAYMENT
			+
			=

Breakdown of Savings

These items are also called sinking funds. These are the safety nets in your plan.

After fully funding your emergency fund, start saving for other items, like furniture, cars, home maintenance or a vacation. This sheet will remind you that every dollar in your savings account is already committed to something.

Amount you have in each sinking fund

Your target balance for each sinking fund

ITEMS	BALANCE	TARGET
Emergency Fund (1) $1,000		
Emergency Fund (2) 3–6 Months		
Retirement Fund		
College Fund		
Real Estate Taxes		
Homeowner's Insurance		
Repairs/Maintenance Fee		
Replace Furniture		
Car Insurance		
Car Replacement		
Disability Insurance		
Health Insurance		
Doctor		
Dentist		
Optometrist		
Life Insurance		
School Tuition/Supplies		
Gifts (Including Christmas)		
Vacation		
Computer Replacement		
Tires		
Baby		
Other		

Consumer Equity Sheet

Your net worth: what you own minus what you owe.

Use this form to list all of your assets and their value. Then subtract what, if anything, you owe on each one. When you total the columns, the Total Equity box at the bottom shows your net worth.

How much each item is worth

How much you owe on each item

Subtract debt from value to get equity

ITEMS	VALUE	—	DEBT	=	EQUITY
Real Estate _____					
Real Estate _____					
Car _____					
Car _____					
Cash on Hand					
Checking Account					
Savings Account					
Money Market Account					
Mutual Funds					
Retirement Plan					
Cash Value (Insurance)					
Household Items					
Jewelry					
Antiques					
Boat					
Unsecured Debt (Negative)					
Credit Card Debt (Negative)					
Other _____					
Other _____					

This is your net worth

☐ — ☐ = ☐

Lump Sum Payment Form

These items are also called sinking funds. These are the safety nets in your plan.

After fully funding your emergency fund, start saving for other items, like furniture, cars, home maintenance or a vacation. This sheet will remind you that every dollar in your savings account is already committed to something.

When this item comes due, how much will you need to cover it?

Use the formula below to find how much to budget

This amount goes into your monthly budget form

ITEM NEEDED	AMOUNT NEEDED ÷	MONTHS =	BUDGETED
Real Estate Taxes			
Homeowner's Insurance			
Home Repairs			
Replace Furniture			
Medical Bills			
Health Insurance			
Life Insurance			
Disability Insurance			
Car Insurance			
Car Repair/Tags			
Replace Car			
Clothing			
Tuition			
Bank Note			
IRS (Self-Employed)			
Vacation			
Gifts (Including Christmas)			
Other _____			
Other _____			

Major Components

Your financial plan has a lot of moving parts.

So you have to know what you need to do and when you need to do it. This form shows you the essential things that absolutely must be part of any successful plan. Go line by line and note what action you need to take for each item, then put a deadline on it.

ITEM	ACTION NEEDED	ACTION DATE
Written Cash Flow Plan		
Will or Estate Plan		
Debt Reduction Plan		
Tax Reduction Plan		
Emergency Funding		
Retirement Funding		
College Funding		
Charitable Giving		
Teach My Children		
Life Insurance		
Health Insurance		
Disability Insurance		
Auto Insurance		
Homeowner's Insurance		
Renter's Insurance		
Long-Term Care Insurance		
Identity Theft Insurance		

Recommended Percentages

How much of your money should go where?

We've got some recommendations based on experience and research. If you find that you spend much more in one category than we recommend, consider adjusting your lifestyle in that area in order to enjoy more freedom and flexibility across the board. These are only suggestions though. For example, if you have a higher income, your percentage for things like food will be lower.

Use this formula to get your target percentages

Total monthly Income **X** Recommended Percentage

Use this formula to get your actual percentages

Budgeted Amount **÷** Total monthly Income **X** **100**

ITEM	RECOMMENDED %	TARGET	ACTUAL
Charitable Gifts	10–15%		
Saving	10–15%		
Housing	25–35%		
Utilities	5–10%		
Food	5–15%		
Transportation	10–15%		
Clothing	2–7%		
Medical/Health	5–10%		
Insurance	10–25%		
Personal	5–10%		
Recreation	5–10%		
Debts	5–10%		

Income Sources Recap

Money's fun. If you've got some.

You've got money coming in from somewhere, right? Then write it down. This form documents every single income source you've got. There's no such thing as "found money." It all counts, and it all goes on the budget!

Enter the amount of each income item here

Enter the date or pay period it will arrive

EMPLOYMENT	AMOUNT	ARRIVAL DATE
Paycheck 1		
Paycheck 2		
Commissions		
Bonus		
Self-Employment		
Tax Refund		
Other_____		

INVESTMENTS/RETIREMENT		
Interest Income		
Dividend Income		
Rental Income		
Trust Fund		
Social Security		
Pension		
Annuity		
Other_____		

OTHER		
Disability Income		
Alimony		
Child Support		
TANF		
Cash Gifts		
Unemployment		
Other_____		

Add up & enter total Income

Pro Rata Debt List

"But I can't pay the minimum payments!" It's okay. We have a plan for that.

Pro rata means "fair share." Use this form to figure out what percentage of your income each creditor represents, and then send their payment along with a copy of this form and your budget every month—even if they say they won't accept it.

Step 1

Subtract Necessity Expense (**B**) from Household Income (**A**). That gives you your Disposable Income (**C**). That's how much money you have to pay toward debt after you've covered all your necessities.

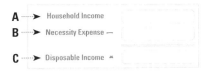

A ----▶ Household Income

B ----▶ Necessity Expense —

C ----▶ Disposable Income =

Step 2

Write in your Total Debt (**D**). Then collect all your bills and add up the grand total of all your monthly minimum payments. Write that in Total Min. Payments (**E**). If your Total Min. Payments figure is higher than your Disposable Income (**C**) figure, you need to use the Pro Rata Debt List.

D ----▶ Total Debt

E ----▶ Total Min. Payments

ITEM	PAYOFF ÷	TOTAL DEBT =	PERCENT X	DISP. INC. =	NEW PMT.
F	G	H	I	J	K

Step 3

List each debt in the Item (**F**) column and write the total debt payoff amount in the Payoff (**G**) column. Go ahead and write in the Total Debt (**H**) and Disposable Income—or Disp. Inc. (**J**)—amounts from the top of the form too.

Step 4

On each line, divide the Payoff (**G**) by the Total Debt (**H**) to get the Percent (**I**). That figure shows you each creditor's fair share of your available income.

Step 5

Multiply the Percent (**I**) by your total disposable income in the Disp. Inc. (**J**) column. Write that in the New Pmt. (**K**) column. That's what you should send to that specific creditor. Repeat that math for every item on the list to calculate your pro rata payments for each one.

Pro Rata Debt List

Don't include consumer debt payments

Add up the total debt column & enter total here

Household Income	
Necessity Expense —	
Disposable Income =	

Total Debt	
Total Min. Payments	

Add up all your minimum payments & enter here

Use the formula below to find your new payment

ITEM	PAYOFF	÷ TOTAL DEBT	= PERCENT	X DISP. INC.	= NEW PMT.

Index